Philosophers
at Table

Philosophers
at Table

On Food and Being Human

Raymond D. Boisvert
and Lisa Heldke

REAKTION BOOKS

Published by Reaktion Books Ltd
Unit 32, Waterside
44–48 Wharf Road
London N1 7UX, UK
www.reaktionbooks.co.uk

First published 2016, reprinted 2016
Transferred to digital printing 2024

Printed and bound in the USA by University of Chicago Press

A catalogue record for this book is available from the British Library

ISBN 978 1 78023 588 2

Contents

Introduction

The How of Eating

'How are we to eat?' The question seems deceptively simple. Its grammatical structure might make it an excellent example to use in an English language textbook to introduce the infinitive, or the use of interrogatives: 'How are we to eat? When are we to eat? Where are we to eat? Why are we to eat?'

Read in another way, it is a question dense with possible interpretations; the perfect frame for a philosophical inquiry into food. If we tease out some of its meanings, we begin to glimpse the ways in which food and philosophy speak to each other. We begin to understand, on the one hand, how philosophy might help us to reflect on the many pressing questions about food that presently swirl around us: whom do we trust to tell us about the safety of our food? How can we address worldwide food insecurity? Is 'local food' always the answer?

We also begin to get a sense of how our relationships to food can help us think about some of the main problems in philosophy. We come to see that 'how are we to eat?' might be one of the deepest, most profound and most 'natural' questions a philosopher could ask – a realization we believe points to the acknowledgement that food is a deeply philosophical subject, and that philosophy is, or can be, a deeply 'foody' activity.

Claims such as these likely seem implausible at first appearance. To begin to understand them as just a bit less kooky and idiosyncratic, consider the word 'how', in the question 'how are we to eat?' Consider the ways its meaning shifts depending on who voices it. It might be an elderly couple who find themselves stranded in a freak snowstorm while travelling on a remote wilderness road; or a kosher-keeping Jew attending an important, very public banquet, who finds that the main dish mixes meat and dairy; or perhaps a new schoolteacher watching her students fling the school's flavourless, nutritionally marginal food into the bin, and wondering how they can learn if they are not better fed. Or it might be an old-school, old-world grandmother teaching table manners to her SpongeBob generation grandchildren. Is the questioner a Western guest struggling to be decorous with unfamiliar eating utensils at dinner in a private home in China? Or a parent of three children, all of whom participate in after-school activities? One can easily imagine any of these people asking 'How – just how – are we to eat?' in varying tones of desperation, piety, curiosity, righteous indignation or gustatory dismay, their version of the question arising out of concerns about everything from health to cultural appropriateness.

The intensity of this question in its various versions declares what we know, implicitly, to be the case: food is a fundamental source of meaning and value in human life. Indeed, food is a fundamental source of human life itself. The question 'how are we to eat?' asks, among other things, how (practically) shall we gather our food? How (nutritionally) should we compose a meal? How ought we honour our deepest (ethical) commitments with our dietary choices? How can we cultivate (aesthetic) taste by cultivating our palate? How (physically) should we care for ourselves through our food choices? How (ecologically) do we exercise our responsibilities to the rest of the living world through those choices? How (educationally) do we instruct the next generation about the importance of food? How (culturally) do we interact with others whose beliefs are different from our own? How, in the end, can we *know* (epistemologically) that our decisions about what (ontologically) to eat make good, human sense?

This book sets out from the premise that exploring the question 'how are we to eat?' is a project that deserves serious philosophical attention. In this introduction, we frame the project by first saying a bit about what we mean by 'philosophy', and then a bit about what we mean by 'food'.

Philosophy as Plumbing

People think of philosophy as a special and rather grand subject cut off from others, something you could put on the mantelpiece. I think it is much more like plumbing . . .
Mary Midgley[1]

Lisa's friend Bruce's email was plaintive. Just back from a glorious holiday in Spain, he and his partner Landis were entertaining four members of Landis's family in their tiny Los Angeles house, which was also, inconveniently, undergoing a major renovation project: 'Nuts here. Landis's relatives are visiting, sleeping on floors, etc., it's hot, AND OUR SEWER PIPE IS BROKEN AND WE HAVE NO SHOWERS OR TOILETS! I'm about to lose it.'

The scene wasn't difficult to imagine. Six full-grown people – two of them American teenagers who would, under the best of circumstances, find the quarters cramped – now suddenly find themselves unable to escape to the only room in the house where they should have been able to find sanctuary in the form of uninterrupted privacy, a cool shower and gastro-intestinal relief. All of it gone, in a burst pipe.

The net: plumbing matters. Civilizations rise and fall because of their ability or inability to provide their citizens with fresh water (essential) and to carry away waste (essential plus). The ancient Romans are remembered still for the magnificence of their plumbing. Remnants of Roman aqueducts grace the landscape in the south of France and are visited each year by large numbers of tourists, who marvel that these beautiful structures also served such a valuable utilitarian purpose. The latrines and baths of the ancient Roman port city of Ostia are among the most visited and most commented-on features of those vast, remarkable ruins. In contemporary middle-class America, if you run out of hot water midway through your shower on a cold morning you won't die, but chances are that you'll begin your day in a crabby mood.

Plumbing matters so much to humans, in part, because every day of our lives we must both consume water in order to keep from dying of dehydration, and produce waste to keep from poisoning ourselves. We perform these tasks using Byzantine sets of pipes and valves, faucets and couplings that, for the most part, remain hidden behind walls and beneath gardens. In modern society, the miracle of plumbing (and it *is* a miracle in every secular sense of that word) operates behind the scenes, quietly guaranteeing that both of those needs – along with a host of others that range from the vital (drinking water) to the frivolous (fountains in Las Vegas) – can be served on demand. A properly functioning plumbing system enables clean water to enter and dirty water to exit, all without fuss or muss. Punch through the sewer main with a post hole digger, and you've got nothing but fuss and – guaranteed – a great deal of muss.

A plumbing disaster can take days to repair and entail major costs. Despite that fact, you may still ignore all the early warning signs of an impending disaster in your home. Indeed, for many of us, avoidance and evasion are the most frequently used tools in our home repair kits. For how long did that bath drain slowly? When did you first notice that drip under the kitchen sink? Has there always been this damp, squishy spot in the lawn? What's that funny smell? Let's not worry about it; it's probably nothing. We do nothing in part because we know that what begins as a small plumbing repair task often ends up as a huge, costly, complicated plumbing overhaul. On the other hand, if we just leave things alone, we can probably limp along for a good long time. (This is certainly what Bruce and Landis experienced – at least until it all went south that hot day in LA when their sewer main exploded.) Plumbing and sewerage systems are so completely entwined in buildings and municipalities that it is no small matter to start over and replace one in its entirety; only the very desperate would likely consider such a move.

So why does the philosopher Mary Midgley suggest that philosophy is a lot like plumbing – an idea that she admits 'has sometimes been thought rather undignified'?[2] Midgley identifies a surprisingly long list of commonalities between the two domains, of which three are the most important: first, in 'elaborate cultures', both are 'fairly complex system[s] . . . usually unnoticed, but which sometimes [go] wrong'. Second, both serve 'vital needs' and are 'hard to repair' because 'neither of them was ever consciously planned as a whole.' Third, when they break or malfunction, 'there have been many ambitious attempts to reshape both of them. But, for both, existing complications are usually too widespread to allow a completely new start.'[3]

Midgley notes that, just as we are likely to try to ignore plumbing problems for as long as we can, so too do we ignore philosophical problems. But here lies one difference between philosophy and plumbing: when the blockage is of a philosophical variety, it is possible to ignore and even deny it for much longer than when your kitchen sink backs up. One can create workarounds that mask a philosophical problem, and even deny altogether that there is a problem. Philosophical problems 'just quietly distort and obscure our thinking'.[4] So quiet are they, and so systematic their distortion, in fact, that we may do much more than just deny that our system has a problem; we may deny the very existence of a philosophical system operating in our lives that *could* malfunction. This is not a problem with our concepts, it is just reality: the way things are.

Philosophical plumbing shapes the ways we encounter and interrogate our world. It circumscribes what count as valid and invalid questions, but it often goes unnoticed, mistaken for 'good old common sense' or 'the way things are'. Philosophical plumbing actually shapes the very questions we are able to ask – and virtually guarantees the problems we will encounter. It makes other questions unaskable – and other problems unimaginable, unformable, because of the shape the system takes. For instance, if your philosophical plumbing system defines minds as sharply different from bodies, one of the problems you are guaranteed to have to work out is the problem of how those two substances communicate with each other. On the other hand, you will have a much easier time arguing for the persistence of the soul after the death of the body; two utterly different substances clearly are not so interdependent that the death of one necessarily results in the death of the other.

People do not generally deny their reliance on plumbing. Many people, on the other hand, do insist that philosophy is of no relevance to their lives. Furthermore, people using malfunctioning philosophical systems are likely to find allies – others, that is, who are equally wedded to that system. The assent of those others helps make plausible the idea that the system *is* working; there is a kind of legitimacy in numbers. When it comes to philosophical systems, if you can surround yourself with people who experience the world as you do, you can probably insulate yourself for quite some time even from potentially debilitating problems with your philosophical system.[5] This is perhaps nowhere truer than in the community of academic philosophers, who can attend conferences of, and write papers for, like-minded thinkers, and can shield themselves from the views of 'ordinary people' by using obscure, technical vocabularies and arcane bodies of textual evidence. It's our *job* to make our philosophical systems plausible to ourselves. (And over the centuries, we have made some pretty implausible philosophies sound pretty plausible to ourselves.)

Adherents of malfunctioning philosophical systems are also likely to find aspects of existence – aspects of what we like to call 'reality' – that support or reinforce their favourite systems. For instance, if you are looking for it, you can find plenty of evidence that thinking is an activity that is carried out by a mind utterly independent from a physical body. (In contrast, try to persuade someone that there is plenty of evidence that the hot water tap isn't dripping in the kitchen.)

Midgley suggests that when an individual's thinking does malfunction to the point that they are finally forced to notice it, they 'find it much easier to look for the source of trouble outside [themselves] than within'; it can be extremely hard to 'turn our attention to what might be wrong in the structure of our thought'.[6] What goes for the individual goes even more strongly for a civilization or society as a whole. In a path-breaking book in the philosophy of science, *The Copernican Revolution* (1957), the philosopher Thomas Kuhn argued that Copernicus's contemporaries preferred to patch up Ptolemy's theory of planetary motion, rather than adopt Copernicus's far more drastic 'fix', which required rejecting a crucial belief that the sun and the planets all revolve around the earth. Too much rested upon that view; discarding it could be nothing other than hopelessly complicated.

Replacing, or even significantly remodelling, a philosophical system, is incredibly difficult. It can be daunting, humbling and exhausting enough just to tear down the walls that must be removed to *expose* the Byzantine network of pipes and valves that serve as a culture's philosophical system. It is even more daunting to replace the damaged section of thinking, to reroute the system around it, or (most drastically) to start in the middle of things to fundamentally transform the system. We would rather continue to use familiar concepts, ways of thinking and beliefs, even when they are doing a terrible job of helping us get along in our world – a task which *should* be one of the central things we can rely on our philosophies to provide us. We soldier on with our old concepts at least in part because it's simply too disruptive and upsetting to try to repair or replace them; the roles they perform in our lives are as vital to us as the processes of conveying fresh water and carrying away waste. To a tremendous degree, they define us; they explain to us who we are, and to remove them would be so disorienting that we might literally be unable to function.

And that, in turn, is because philosophical concepts are so comprehensive in their scope and application. Think here of plumbing, heating and cooling, electricity and your credit card: now imagine if all those systems in your home life began to act up simultaneously. That is what it can be like to have a crisis in your philosophical system, because philosophical ideas, concepts and positions (about, for example, what it means to be a good person, about what it even means to be a human being, about how we can ever know anything about the world in which we find ourselves, about whether there is or isn't some larger plan at work in the cosmos) run through so many aspects of our everyday life that, when we begin to doubt one of them, it can throw everything in our lives into disarray. Consider – or remember – what your life would be like were you suddenly to have deep, fundamental misgivings about what it means to be a decent human being; imagine how this would lead you to falter and stumble over every decision, every action you needed to take in your life. Midgley writes that 'the patterns underlying our thought are much more powerful, more intricate and more dangerous than we usually notice . . . they need constant attention, and . . . no one of them is a safe universal guide.'[7] If we acknowledge that our world's conceptual complexity always shifts under us, that it requires us to tend it and that it can never be entirely relied upon to serve us in our daily lives, we might also come to acknowledge that there is a role for philosophy – and philosophers – in that world. We *need* the activity of philosophy because we 'live in a constant, and constantly increasing, conceptual mess, and . . . we need to do something about it.' 'There are', Midgley says, 'limits to living in a mess.'[8]

Bruce and Landis hit the plumbing-mess limit the day Landis's family came to visit. Until that day, they were living in a house with a sewerage system that was – unbeknown to them – a functional mess. When there were just two adults in the house, the mess remained literally below the surface, undetectable to ordinary users of the home. But when four more water-using adults – four more complicating factors – entered the system, it collapsed under the stress, making the undetectable mess immediately, unavoidably evident.

Conceptual messes sometimes present themselves to us with this level of insistence; more often, however, they are of the 'slow-draining bath' variety. They allow us to function well enough that there's little incentive to get to the bottom of them. But the effects of a few small, persistent messes can, eventually, be equally unavoidable. Eventually, even long-standing beliefs have to be replumbed when they become too clogged.

What sort of activity is philosophy? That is, how does it reroute, repair and replace the pipes that form our systems for living in, experiencing and being part of the world? Midgley suggests that the philosopher – at least the great philosopher whose work continues to matter in the world – is a combination of poet and lawyer: 'They must have both the new vision that points the way we are to go and the logical doggedness that sorts out just what is, and what is not, involved in going there.'[9] Vision without logical doggedness is ineffectual daydreaming; logical doggedness without vision is arcane scholasticism irrelevant to the activity of living.

On this view philosophy is not the repository of absolute truths, nor is it the creator of grand metanarratives. It is an activity of identifying clogs, breaks and other sorts of problems in our conceptual schemes, and creating conceptual tools that enable us to repair, replace or otherwise render those schemes functional again. Here is where the work of the philosopher – the work of poetry and law, of vision and dogged logic – begins: in the midst of the problems of real life, where the conceptual confusions pool at the surface like the contents of a burst water main.

Midgley rejects the assertion that philosophy of this sort is 'applied philosophy', as if it were a 'mere by-product of the pure kind – a secondary spin-off from nobler, more abstract processes going on in ivory towers'.[10] Such a view of philosophy predominates in many philosophical circles as well as in the popular consciousness. Philosophy in this view has nothing to do with the ordinary world, and nothing to do with practical matters. It is pure speculation about matters of the highest level of abstraction – God, time, truth, beauty. Insofar as these are philosophical concepts, their everyday meanings must be set aside. Never mind that such concepts actually have everything to do with the everyday world – what is the discussion of beauty if it is disconnected from all discussion of beautiful things, for example?

Midgley points out that the great philosophers – figures such as Socrates and Kant, who are regarded as paradigmatic practitioners of philosophy – all began their inquiries by 'diving straight into the moral, political, religious and scientific problems arising' in their own times. Only then did they 'move on towards abstraction, not for its own sake, but because it was needed in order to clear up the deeper confusions underlying these primary messes'.[11] Philosophy begins in wonder, Midgley would agree, but it is wonder of a very grounded sort, as in, 'I wonder what we should have for dinner tonight; I wonder which batch of nutritional advice I should follow. And I wonder why current public discussion about nutrition is so schismatic, separating those who want to talk about nutritional components *of* foods from those who want to think about nutrition in a holistic sense. I wonder how this schism relates to other schisms in our world – about religion, for instance, or about what a family is.' Explore a real-life conceptual confusion and you will likely find a larger, deeper, philosophical confusion.

Such philosophy does not *begin* with abstraction and produce practical solutions for our everyday messes only as a derivative industry. Everyday life messes are both the sources of, and the 'final projects' for, philosophy. Such philosophy is engaged in the work of creating what Susanne Langer calls new 'generative ideas'; that is, of reconceptualizing familiar facts under new principles that will, in turn, incline us to reformulate still other facts.[12] Elsewhere she says that philosophy is 'the continual pursuit of meanings – wider, clearer, more negotiable, more articulate meanings'.[13] In Langer's formulation we can hear her emphasis on the importance of ideas engaging with our everyday world; we pursue meanings not just because they are beautiful in the abstract (which they might well be), but because we seek 'wider, clearer, more negotiable' meanings.

Midgley's rejection of 'applied philosophy' also echoes the attitude of an earlier philosopher, the American pragmatist John Dewey, who argued that the distinction between applied and 'pure' philosophy, as well as applied and pure science, was rooted in a conceptual misunderstanding that historically has had disastrous consequences.[14] Dewey suggested that advances in 'pure' science actually emerge out of – and ultimately ought to reconnect to – concrete problems of life. He called them 'so many cases of science-in-action' and wrote that 'the important thing is that [a scientific fact] be grasped in its social connections – its function in life.'[15]

Dewey would go one step further than Midgley to reject not only the hierarchical distinction between pure and applied theorizing, but the related ontological distinction between minds and bodies – a distinction that draws a sharp separation between humans as minds and the 'external' ('material') world we describe with our theories. The notion that the world is external – or that we are external to the world – is another misapprehension, an effect of a particular system of philosophical plumbing on which minds and bodies are considered fundamentally different kinds of substances. For many of us, the idea of an 'internal' mind and an 'external' world feels like common sense – like an accurate description of the way things 'really' are. But it is in fact a by-product of a particular philosophical system. On an alternative system – one we are advocating here – humans are in the world and of the world, in the same way as are the corn and the soil in which that corn grows. Human inquiry is not *itself* interior to humans' minds; inquiry is a part of the world in which it takes place, and it has the power to transform that world.

Building upon this understanding of philosophy and the world, we would further argue that the philosopher must be more than just a poet and a lawyer. Poetry and law can incline towards just the sort of disembodied abstraction we seek to avoid, even when their practitioners might be writing sonnets about cattle and chickens, or drawing up binding agreements about literal bodies of land. The philosopher thus needs to be identified with a third kind of occupation, one that is fundamentally engaged with the (so-called 'material') world in a way that renders it difficult if not impossible to preserve a self/world or theory/practice separation. The third occupation ought to be one whose practitioners engage in their world in a manner we could characterize as 'thoughtful practice', or 'reflective handwork'.

One ideal candidate for this occupation is the farmer. To the poet's vision and the lawyer's logical doggedness, the farmer adds the understanding that the work of reflection, exploration and speculation must eventually go to ground (literally) in the form of a crop. The farmer recognizes that the most visionary yet logical conceptual scheme in the world is worth nothing if it is not *in* the world, incarnated (literally) in humans' experiential lives.

The farmer is particularly appropriate because her activity serves one of humankind's most fundamental needs, which is also one of humans' greatest pleasures: the need for food. Eating is (better, eating *can be*) a deeply integrative activity, weaving together natural products, human artisans, creativity, nutrition, sociability, even reverence. The farmer can be creative or utilitarian, can place primary emphasis on either need or pleasure. But what she can never be is utterly disembodied. The farmer's chicken can never be just a figure of speech. Farming is an activity in the service of human survival that is also deeply creative; it is this vital connection between human necessity and human creativity that we invoke in making the farmer the third aspect of the philosopher.

Food as Philosophical

We return now to the question with which we began: how are we to eat? Armed with an understanding of philosophy as, in part, a thoughtful practice designed for cleaning up messes, we might now be attuned to hear in the question an acknowledgement that food is messy in just such a sense. To ask 'how are we to eat?' is, in part, to admit that we're having trouble feeding ourselves. How are we to eat, given global warming, water pollution, desertification and topsoil loss? How are we to eat, confronted with the nutritionally poor choices on supermarket shelves and school lunch lines; or with the contamination of elemental foodstuffs, like spinach, peanuts and apples? How to eat when healthcare costs far outpace wages and buying cheap food is one way to cut corners? How, when we recall the many in the world who face chronic malnourishment and undernourishment, or the many (human and non-human) animals whose lives are literally endangered in the production of our diets? On the more recreational end of things, how are we to eat when the variety and quality of our options overwhelms us and we literally cannot choose where or what to eat (Thai tonight? Peruvian? Homemade comfort food?); when the sheer number of our choices derails us? When we believe we are too fat, according to some measure that matters to us; when others declare us too fat; when the prescriptions of 'experts' about food and health shift beneath us, and conflict with each other?

The food life of a contemporary inhabitant of the United States (to take the country with which the authors are most familiar) contains any number of messes, ranging from the economic to the environmental, the cultural and to the health-related. The messes that entangle you may be very different from those that enmesh your neighbour; your economic status, your race and ethnicity, your gender, your size, your age and your level of health will all contribute to determining which messes in our large systems affect you most directly. If you have a peanut allergy or celiac disease, you care about honest food labelling in a way far different from someone who is just trying to ensure she gets enough fibre in her diet every day. If you are feeding a family on a modest income, you are acutely aware of how much it would cost to fill half your plate with vegetables and fruits.

In order to get through the day, we are likely going to choose to avert our gaze from many of these messes. They don't rise to the level of catastrophe in our lives, and so we can choose not to think about them. Who cares whether the pad thai packet is really 'authentic' or not? It's not *too* expensive, the kids love it, and you can have it on the table within twenty minutes of getting home from work. Strike 'cultural authenticity mess' from the list of things worrying you. In contrast, if you're a meat eater and are throwing some chicken into that pad thai, you may want to double down on 'meat safety mess', especially if there are small children in your household: this is a mess that can have literally life-threatening consequences. Drinking milk? The artificial growth hormone it contains that you're consuming may or may not have consequences for human health – you may just have to wait and see on that one. Given the presence of those small children, you'll probably be buying some apples (kid-friendly, affordable snack food), and thereby must make some kind of decision about how to negotiate the conceptual mess of local and/or organic. In short, to live (and thus to eat) in the contemporary world is to negotiate a treacherous set of conceptual sinkholes, some of which threaten to drown you, while others risk only damp feet.

The point of this book is not to 'fix' any of these messes in the forms in which they have bubbled to the surface, nor to replace the work on food being done by researchers, physicians, nutritionists, cooks and farmers. In the case of every kind of issue we have mentioned, repair is a job better done by experts in other, specialized, fields – and chances are, it's also already being done. Philosophers' training does not equip them with any of the specialized knowledges that are needed to 'solve' concrete problems in the ways our food is grown, processed, transported, cooked and disposed of. Nor does our profession equip us to assess matters of diet, health and nutrition.

Of what use is the philosopher in cleaning up our food messes, then? Addressing that question is the task of this book, but a preliminary answer is in order here. The contributions of philosophy can be sorted into several interrelated tasks. First, the philosopher looks for conceptual and terminological commonalities among the messes that confront us: where do we find similar words cropping up within disparate food movements? (Consider in how many food arenas the following words appear: 'authentic', 'sustainable', 'choice'.) Do the words lead back to some of the same generative ideas, despite arising in different contexts? What can we learn by exploring the commonalities among them? Concepts emerge as junction points, bringing together ideas that may seem diverse and disparate. The fermentation expert Sandor Katz discusses his favourite example of such a conceptual node in his book *The Art of Fermentation* (2012): the word 'culture.'[16] This word crops up inside the word 'agriculture'; it refers to the process by which you ferment or 'sour' a food like milk; and it of course refers to a set of beliefs, practices and world views that hold together a group of people – 'the totality of all that humans seek to pass from generation to generation', as Katz puts it.[17] Katz points out that these arenas can seem quite disconnected from each other, but if we hold them in creative connection (through, among other things, the expedient of an etymological root), we can notice important features of each that we might not have otherwise:

> In fact, the word *culture* comes from Latin *cultura*, a form of *colere*, 'to cultivate.' Our cultivation of the land and its creatures – plants, animals, fungi, and bacteria – is essential to culture. Reclaiming our food and our participation in cultivation is a means of cultural revival . . .
>
> This is not just about fermentation . . . but about food more broadly. Every living creature on this Earth interacts intimately with its environment via its food. Humans in our developed technological society, however, have largely severed this connection, and with disastrous results.[18]

For Katz, reviving the culturing of food can actually revive and reinvigorate human culture: its creativity, its economic systems, its relations to the environment and so on. Whether or not one agrees with Katz's intriguing thesis about the power of a pickle to change our society, the power of his work lies in the ways it invites us to see 'culture' in a new, more complex way.

Second, and relatedly, the philosopher identifies underlying, unstated assumptions that are at work in our various conceptual systems. What is the relationship between these assumptions and the messes in which we find ourselves? We will make use of Langer's term 'generative idea' to carry out this second kind of work. We focus in particular on tracing the generative ideas that coalesced into what has come to be known as the modern era – a term that refers to the ways of thinking that emerged in Europe during the period between the Renaissance and the early nineteenth century. Many of the modern generative ideas or assumptions on which we focus take the form of fundamental dichotomies: between mind and body, between theory and practice, between reason and emotion. How does our inattentive, even unknowing devotion to these dichotomous assumptions 'help' lead us into the kinds of food messes in which we presently find ourselves?

Building upon these two tasks, the third task of philosophy is to ask what we might call 'questions of reorientation': questions that bring into focus those assumptions, principles and concepts so as to begin to ask 'how else might we go about this?' (In Langer's terms, this is about coming up with new generative ideas.) What would happen if we shifted our assumptions or our starting point? This third task is the very heart of our project. The reorienting question that shapes our investigation is this: what happens if we begin philosophical inquiry with the acknowledgement that we are hungry beings – that food and our relationships to it are unbracketable features of human life, and therefore features of which philosophy must take account? A second reorienting question follows from the first: what if we were to begin from an understanding of humans as 'stomach-endowed' beings, rather than as 'minds that happen to be housed in bodies' (which is the slightly cartoonish way we might state the modern understanding of what it is to be a human being). Other questions that follow reconsider the various dichotomous assumptions that are our modern inheritance. For instance, how might we reconceive the theory/practice dichotomy if we take food-making activities seriously – activities that are not well understood using such a dichotomy?

We would make two observations about the way in which we've described the tasks of philosophers. First, and most obviously, we do not mean to suggest that only 'card-carrying' philosophers can do philosophy or be philosophical. Quite the contrary; it is our contention that philosophy is everywhere, and thus that practitioners of every discipline, as well as all persons in their everyday lives as consumers, family members and community participants, regularly engage in the work of philosophy. This is as it should be. Professional philosophers are distinct in that we are the ones who consciously take it as our particular charge to ensure that philosophical tasks are actually carried out; it is our job, literally, in the way that it is not the job of the farmer, grocer, cook or eater, nor the job of the dairy scientist, agronomist or economist. Because it is really our full-time job, we ought to be expected to be consistently good at it, in just the way one ought to expect a major league baseball player to catch the ball almost every time. But notice some things that this analogy with baseball reveals. First, while major leaguers are consistently and as a group far more skilful than ten-year-olds, it is possible for professional players to play very poorly, and for kids to make spectacular plays. This is perhaps even truer in the philosophical arena, where young children quite regularly make observations of stunning philosophical lucidity (and, let it be added, professionals say things that are undeniably foolish). Children may not be able to develop sophisticated arguments to support those observations, but their beauty and clarity are not diminished because of that.

The second thing this analogy reveals is that there is a continuity between the game played in the Little League and that played in the big leagues, such that a player at one level would recognize the game being played at another level *as baseball*. With respect to philosophy, it may be that not all participants recognize that activity over there as 'doing philosophy' in the same way that ball players would pick up on four bases and a bat. The fault for this should perhaps be laid at the door of professional philosophy itself, which has tended to take a certain 'don't try this at home' attitude towards its own activity, sometimes acting as if there is no connection between barstool musings and the presidential address at the American Philosophical Association. We beg to differ – and write this book in part in an effort to make that everyday philosophy more apparent.

The second observation we would make about our understanding of the task of philosophers is this: our definition of philosophy has studiously avoided asserting that its task is to uncover 'underlying truths' or 'overarching principles' or 'absolutes'. While philosophy has often historically been seen – both by philosophers and by the 'outside world' – as the quest for Truth (where the capital T tells you it's the real McCoy), we identify our own lineage in a different branch of that history. Philosophy is indeed a 'love of wisdom', as its Greek etymology suggests, but 'wisdom' does not mean fixed and unchanging Ideas. And 'love' is not a passive state but a constant effort; it is a perpetual seeking. In keeping with our understanding of philosophy as concerned with realizing meaning in the midst of things, we emphasize the always provisional nature of the meanings it develops. Philosophy of food, then, is not the work of identifying fixed and unchanging moral laws to govern our eating habits, or absolute aesthetic principles to use in evaluating all dining experiences everywhere. Just as you cannot carry out a plumbing repair that will last forever, neither can the philosopher develop concepts that will never need changing.

The Organization of this Book

Philosophers at Table reconsiders the major fields of philosophical inquiry by using the question 'how are we to eat?' as a focusing device. That question can be read as a version of the reorienting question we noted earlier: what happens when we begin philosophical inquiry with the acknowledgement that we are hungry beings? The philosophy of food as we conceive it is as much an investigation of philosophy as it is of food. Starting philosophy from humans' interests in and needs for food can, we believe, contribute to the transformation of philosophy into an activity that more fully speaks to human life.

This book begins with ethics, the philosophical field in which questions about food might seem most likely to arise. Our examination in Chapter One begins at the dinner table, with the question of what a hospitable host is supposed to do when faced with a table full of guests, each of whom has particular dietary needs, demands and predilections. What does hospitality 'demand' of us? Our examination of this often neglected virtue places it at the centre of ethical inquiry. When hospitality is a model virtue, the dichotomies that have often dominated Western ethics (good/bad, right/wrong, evil/beneficial) are replaced with clusters of possibilities, many of which exist in tension with each other. Tensions are not automatically and always problems; they are, however, ordinary features of the world in which we live. They cannot be resolved by appeals to absolute, fixed moral laws (there is no 'one right answer' to the question 'how shall I accommodate my various dinner guests' demands and requests?'); rather, tensions are things we learn to live with by creating situation-specific, reasonable accommodations.

One answer to the question 'how are we to eat?' might be: 'with pleasure'. In Chapter Two, the pleasures of the table make their way to the centre of things by way of a discussion of the nature of taste. Consider: we may refer to the capacity for appreciating fine art by the word 'taste', but philosophers have always located that capacity far away from the mouth. Aesthetic taste requires dispassionate objectivity – aesthetic distance – and, ideally, the sequestered setting of a museum. By contrast, literal taste is an undeniably bodily activity, implicated in all the unreliability normally associated with bodies; it's personal, indeed intimate; it's of immediate significance and is part of our everyday activities. This exploration of taste serves the larger purpose of this chapter, which is to offer a reworking of the concepts of art and the aesthetic that decentres the museum and the concert hall. Our alternative conception of art focuses on setting, artistry and the idea of a 'consummatory experience'.

Chapter Three challenges another philosophical dichotomy that has featured prominently in the West: the dichotomy between facts and values. Beginning at the table, with questions about how we are to eat, such a dichotomy seems forced, artificial and unhelpful. We also challenge the primacy of vision as a metaphor for understanding. This chapter explores the question 'how are we to eat?', rewritten as 'how are we to *know* that our decisions about what to eat make sense?' The answer – encoded in our very biological classification – is 'experimentally, thoughtfully, wisely, judiciously. By tasting.' The Latin name *Homo sapiens* underscores our identity as the tasting species. The verb *sapere* means both 'to taste' and 'to think or discern'. Members of *Homo sapiens* are those who reflect upon what they eat. How are we to eat? By tasting/testing, by experimenting and exploring – and then starting over. Philosophers typically associate knowing with seeing, a distancing sense that keeps the known object at least an arm's length away. The ideal inquiry situation, in this association, understands the knowing subject as a detached, neutral observer perceiving an object directly and without distortion in a clear, white light. When we conceive of inquiry along the model of tasting, we move in a different direction altogether. Inquiry-as-tasting suggests an activity characterized first by interestedness, not detachment. Second, the general situation is one of tentativeness, exploration, willingness to reassess one's ideas. Thinking-as-tasting (as opposed to thinking-as-seeing) suggests an intimacy between knower and known – a physical commingling that challenges received views about the relationships between objectivity, dispassion and distance.

Chapter Four addresses metaphysics, commonly considered to be the most abstract, esoteric and – somewhat ironically – fundamental branch of philosophy. It is the branch concerned with questions about the nature of being. Here, the answer to the question 'how are we to eat?' is 'as if our being depended upon it.' A mighty and well-sedimented philosophical axiom holds that 'being is self-sufficient.' When we pay attention to food and how our being *depends* on it, an entirely new framework emerges. The altered framework admits, accepts, indeed welcomes beings' dependences and interdependences. Try to disguise or hide it as we may, we are *needy*. We require food, which in turn means that we need sunshine and rain. We depend on the earthworms and ants that work the soil; the bacteria that keep it fertile; and on the people who raise and harvest crops, slaughter animals and transport, store and distribute food. Such realizations overturn the old hierarchy of being that placed autonomy at the peak and dependence at the nadir. Interdependence can no longer be dismissed as a baser mode of being. How are we to eat? Only with the help of vast numbers of other, equally needy beings.

The sub-discipline of metaphysics, or what is often its synonym, ontology, asks general questions about the nature of things; in particular, 'how do we describe the world in ways that will best enable us to make sense of, and operate in, our surroundings?' The answers that will serve needy beings are vastly different from the answers that would be needed by beings who see themselves as autonomous and self-sufficient. With this acknowledgement, our inquiry into 'how are we to eat?' comes full circle, as metaphysics touches back to ethics. How are we needy beings to eat? Hospitably, with the full knowledge that our lives quite literally rest upon the lives of myriad others.

I

Hospitality is Ethics

Rigid Hosts or Picky Eaters?

'It's becoming harder for Americans to break bread together.'
That, at least, was how the journalist Jessica Bruder reported it.[1]
What made it so hard to eat with others? Too many individualized food preferences. These can wreak havoc for even the most
skilled host. One guest will not eat shellfish. Another, who favours
the paleo diet, insists on meat. A third is a committed vegetarian.
Yet another, frightened after reading an article with the ominous
title 'Is this the Most Dangerous Food for Men?'[2] refuses soy
products. An obligation to ask about preferences, convictions
and allergies has become a major part of what it means to host a
dinner. Nowadays, Bruder suggests, responsible hosts must ask
their guests for a list of their meal requirements, and design their
dinner menus accordingly.

It was not always thus. The Danish writer Isak Dinesen
(pen name of Karen Blixen, 1885–1962) wrote the wonderful
short story 'Babette's Feast', which in turn became a classic 'food
movie' in 1987. Set in the late nineteenth century, the story follows
Babette, a talented French chef exiled as a political refugee to a
remote Danish village. The villagers are mostly members of a particularly austere religious community, whose diet is composed of
something called 'ale-bread soup'. When Babette wins the French
lottery, she decides to spend her winnings by preparing a lavish
meal for the community that welcomed her. She makes all the

plans. Not once does she ask herself 'what should I avoid? What might the members of this community not wish to eat?' Asking such questions would, after years of making ale-bread soup, represent an unacceptable compromise. The villagers' collective palate is not only austere, it is unrefined. Babette's artistic talents as a chef would not be exercised if she adjusted her menu to fit their narrow, deeply doctrinaire tastes. It is the guests, not the chef, who need to adjust.

That the guests need to expand their horizons to meet the capacities of the chef is a fact brought into focus by the presence of another guest, a well-travelled military man, who has in fact eaten Babette's cooking before, at her renowned restaurant in Paris. His obvious enjoyment and appreciation of her artistry is met first with some shock by the other guests, but then, as the wine lubricates them, with something approaching acknowledgement. Although before the dinner commences the guests announce to each other that they will display no pleasure whatsoever in the food they eat, eventually, in the face of the military man's pleasure and their own intoxication, they give over to the delights of the meal.

What's a host to do? The contrast between the situation Bruder describes and the dinner scene in 'Babette's Feast' well illustrates the mess in which contemporary hosts find themselves. To call it a mess is not to argue that allergies do or do not matter. It is rather to notice a shift in the locus of responsibility. For Babette, guests bear responsibility for openness, flexibility and a willingness to adjust in light of a menu prepared by the chef/ host. No less a contemporary food personality than Michael Pollan shares that view. He tends to 'agree with the French, who gaze upon any personal dietary prohibition as bad manners'.[3] Such a perspective is today in full retreat. It is more and more the host who must assume responsibility and adjust. This shift makes sense to us in the contemporary West. After all, we now know a lot more about food allergies than we did in Dinesen's time – and, arguably, we are experiencing a lot more of them than did the inhabitants of Babette's remote religious community. No peanuts; that's for sure. In addition, culturally conscientious hosts will wish to honour their guests' religious convictions; in some cases, pork would probably be a bad entrée choice. Finally, good hosts may well want to make their guests 'ecologically comfortable'. If genetically modified plants, dairy products, meats or foods shipped long distances will offend, these items will have to be excluded.

At the same time, some people are just picky eaters. Others have an unrefined palate. Certain eaters are given to faddishness, while others are simply intransigent and inflexible. Is it really so unreasonable for a guest simply to adjust, politely and out of consideration for others, to whatever menu the host put significant effort into preparing?

On one hand picky eaters, on the other rigid hosts. Where does the burden of responsibility lie? When allergies or children's health are involved, the obligations are fairly clear: guests should be sure that their hosts know about their allergies, and both guest and host must make doubly, triply sure to avoid those allergens.

Once we move beyond life-and-death health concerns, responsibility becomes tougher to assign. Who bears the responsibility for enabling a dinner guest to live out – in this meal – his or her commitment to vegetarianism or Hinduism, or a guest's belief that genetically modified organisms are spiritually unhealthy? Must the hostess whose budget typically takes her to chain supermarkets spend a lot more than usual because several of her guests are locavores? Must a lone paleo dieter insist that the menu include meat? Things can get inconsiderate – not to mention cumbersome – in a hurry. Jessica Bruder's article, for instance, tells the story of guests who contacted a hostess on the very day of her event, to say 'they were vegetarian, vegan or gluten free'.[4] And how and where does the host's responsibility end? Should an administrative assistant feel obliged to honour a co-worker's blunt request that she stock her desktop candy jar (funded by the administrative assistant's own modest salary) with treats that the co-worker's visiting children can eat?

When responsibility shifts – from guest to host, as it seems to have done in the times and places we have described – what brings about that shift? Medical, political and ethical concerns have been around for a long time; they cannot have caused the change all alone. We understand it as an alteration in philosophical assumptions, specifically assumptions about relations between what philosophers have long called 'the one' and 'the many'. Babette's feast illustrates the pre-eminence of 'the one', a unified meal at which guests carry the responsibility of their own dietary needs. Bruder's article illustrates the rise of 'the many', those individual dinner guests whose desires dictate a host's obligations.

This description of the shift in the locus of responsibility takes us into the philosophical field of ethics, the examination of considerations which 'should' guide our lives. Should the guest adjust to the host, or the host to the guest? Some versions of this question can be answered with relative ease. Providing responses that prove adequately justified is a different matter altogether. If we want a consistent, integrated, justifiable way of warranting our decisions, we will need to pay some attention to certain 'big picture' issues, issues such as the relation between the one and the many. Such work is that of neither the specialized sciences nor the social sciences – though the latter might come closer. Philosophy is the field that undertakes this task. It explores and organizes a central cluster of generative ideas that help us get our bearings as we seek to make our way in the world.[5]

The 'Thoughtful Practice' of Ethics

Ethics emerges as an important area of study for philosophy because humans, like other living things, are situated in contexts in which and to which we must be responsive. Predilections and preferences, along with responsibilities, mark the content of ethics. Humans manifest a vast variety of possibilities about what constitutes a good life. We also possess a reflective awareness of that variety. History, anthropology and sociology teach us that, across time and space, cultures have developed remarkably different sets of beliefs and practices about the proper ways to raise children, carry out commerce, organize the state and interact with those defined as 'outsiders'. In one culture, morality dictates that the polite guest is the acquiescent guest. In another, etiquette might demand that the hostess cater to the specific, individual needs of each guest. Options, for the creature with intelligence, necessitate selection. Selection mandates prioritization in terms of the more or less worthy.

Moral philosophy or ethics (we use the terms interchangeably) examines the question of worthiness and culminates in an orientation that can be used to guide our customs and habits. Indeed, the very words 'ethics' and 'morals' come from Greek and Latin roots that mean 'customs' and 'habits'. Because of these origins, one might be tempted to think of ethics as a 'practical' discipline. To some extent, ethics *is* 'practical'. After all, it does culminate in behaviours, habits, customs. At the same time, ethics is something more and other than the practical. It examines the general conditions that occasion discernment and provides some overarching guidance for living out certain options rather than others. In short, it would be inadequate to label ethics as either a purely practical or a purely theoretical activity. The neat either/or oppositions we inherit from the history of Western philosophy simply do not fit our situation as lived. In this significant regard, then, the lived practices which make ethics unavoidable parallel cookery and other 'culinary arts'. Instead of the continual seesaw between theory and practice, these food-centred practices can better be understood as 'thoughtful practices', a phrase that seeks to undercut the theory/practice distinction as it is usually drawn.[6]

The understanding of ethics we develop takes inspiration from the ancient Greek philosopher Aristotle (384–322 BCE). Like Aristotle, we think of ethics as concerning itself with customs and habits, specifically those that help to occasion good lives – that is to say, fruitful, flourishing and meaningful lives. In any given situation we find ourselves confronted with multiple possible responses. For the stomach-attentive philosopher, the responses that are most commendable are those that take account of the full-bodied concreteness of human being (something philosophy has not always done). Such responses will, as Aristotle suggests, combine right feeling, proper reflection and appropriate selection among options. The hoped-for results: humans living good lives.[7]

Despite being one of our heroes, Aristotle tended to overlook food and food practices. Specifically, in his discussion of virtue, he ignores the virtue most closely associated with food – hospitality. Generosity, which he calls 'liberality', is present, but that is as close as he gets. His failure to include hospitality turns out to be the rule among philosophers. This neglect of hospitality can be held responsible for some of the most glaring problems in the history of Western moral philosophy.

Ethics versus Hospitality: Philosophy

Not only has philosophy overlooked hospitality, it has often kept that virtue rigorously separate from ethics. A clear sense of this separation can be found in the thought of Immanuel Kant (1724–1804). Kant specifically contrasts ethics with hospitality in a famous thought experiment – though most accounts of this experiment give short shrift to the hospitality component. The experiment is intended to demonstrate the weight of Kant's major ethical principle: what has come to be called the 'universalizability principle', a version of his 'categorical imperative'.

Kant proposes this principle as a way to resolve sticky, challenging ethical questions. Whenever moral agents confront such questions, Kant directs them to ask a straightforward question: would I want my proposed behaviour to become a universal rule? In other words, would I want a world in which everyone was mandated to act the way I am about to act? This sounds good: it is helpful in difficult situations, it is all about fairness, it makes sure I am paying attention to universal considerations, not self-interest. However, Kant's philosophical opponents were not fully convinced. They highlighted a 'guest example' in their objections.

We would render it this way: An individual is a guest in our home. We know that some people wish this person harm. These people come to our door, armed and angry. They ask if the person is within. What should we do? Must we tell them the truth? Common decency, local custom and the traditions of hospitality urge us to safeguard our guest. Maybe, though, common decency is just another name for 'the easy way out'; perhaps local customs and traditions are outmoded remnants of an age when people were less rational. Remember, the universalizability principle seeks to get beyond local custom and personal preferences. Its aim is to give clear direction by demanding that we consider what happens if we universalize our behaviour. We surely would not want it to become a universal rule that people lie. The ethical mandate is therefore clear, as is the resultant ethical behaviour: we announce, 'yes, the person you seek is hiding in the closet.'

The strength of Kant's position is that he really means business. He allows no wiggle room. Clarity, absoluteness and consistency dominate his ethics. The implications of this position for the subject of hospitality are clear: the absolute demands of ethics trump the flexible customs of hospitality. Ethics is not hospitality; it is, for Kant, a higher obligation that calls on one to eschew even such 'social niceties' as protecting guests from harm when such protection requires one to violate an ethical maxim.

We challenge the view that leads to such a separation and bring the 'food virtue', hospitality, into the centre of ethical consideration. Doing so will occasion a reconsideration of ourselves, our place in the world and our obligations in and to that world. In other words, we will engage in some philosophical reconstruction.

Ethics and Hospitality: Literature

Not every field of thought has eschewed hospitality. Indeed, in many works of literature, hospitality is the very focus of the kind of life that one should lead. The *Inferno*, for instance, portrays hospitality as an obligation, and failure to meet it as evil. Dante (1265–1321) assigns bad hosts to the ninth circle of the Inferno – the lowest circle. Those who fail in their obligations to their guests reside only a bare notch above the very depths of depths, the location occupied by the ultimate traitor, Judas, whose crime might also be understood as a betrayal of hospitality.

A story told by the Roman poet Ovid (43 BCE–*c.* 18 CE) in Book VIII of his *Metamorphoses* points out the value of well-executed hospitality. To understand the story, it is worth noting that it borrows from an older, Greek account, and that Jupiter, the Roman god on whom the story focuses, is known in ancient Greek mythology as Zeus. It is further worth noting that Zeus, chief of the gods, was also called Zeus Xenios, or Zeus, protector of strangers, travellers, supplicants. That's big-time stuff – it means the chief Greek god pays special attention to hospitality, and by extension, so should we.

Ovid's story proceeds in a fairly typical way. Jupiter, accompanied by Mercury, comes to earth in disguise. (If you're a god, there's not much point in showing up as yourself, since everyone will fall all over themselves to be nice to an all-powerful god.) Since they masquerade as beggars, most unsuspecting humans slam their doors in the gods' faces. Not, however, one elderly couple – Baucis and her husband Philemon, who welcome the shabby visitors. Baucis and Philemon realize that hospitality, in the first instance, means providing food. The couple go so far as to plan to kill their only goose in order to prepare an appropriate meal for their guests. Overwhelmed and grateful, the godly guests reveal their identities. They then punish the town's other inhabitants and reward the good Baucis and Philemon by granting their wish that neither die before the other.

Lest one think that Jupiter always comes with beneficent motives, the French playwright Molière (1622–1673) provides a corrective. *Amphitryon*, a comedy typical of Molière, tells the story of the Greek general Amphitryon's heart-rending separation from his young bride. Meanwhile, back home, Jupiter falls prey to an all-too-human lust for that very bride, Alcmene. Being all-powerful, he has a sure-fire technique for seduction: to disguise himself as Amphitryon. Admittedly, as Molière points out, showing up in a bedroom impersonating the husband is not always the best strategy for heightening a wife's lust. In the case of this new marriage, though, Alcmene yearns for Amphitryon. Jupiter gets to enjoy the caresses and ministrations of the lustful, young, beautiful bride. When the real Amphitryon returns, he is surprised by his wife's greeting: 'what, back so soon?' Things then get complicated and, given Molière's deft comedic hand, quite funny.

The stock elements are all here in Molière's play – gods, disguises, unsuspecting mortals – but the ingredients take on a decidedly different form from the story of Baucis and Philemon. Here is a guest who definitely does *not* deserve hospitality. Adding such a story to the mix reveals a baffling dimension of hospitality. First, there is the messy question with which this chapter began: who must adjust to whom – host to guest or guest to host? But Molière's play reveals an even more basic problem faced by the host. Dante's emphasis on obligation notwithstanding, one's duty to guests always requires a degree of discernment. Some guests need to be turned away – otherwise strangers can cause some major Jupiter-style mischief.

That capacity for trouble could explain why the Latin word for stranger, *hostis*, also means 'enemy'. What to do when faced with a stranger? Welcome them or be wary? Despite what we might call the 'Zeus default' (welcome the stranger), there is no fixed formula to provide the guaranteed right answer every time. But, of course, to admit there is no fixed formula seems to violate philosophers' prime directive. Certainly, some philosophers aim at perfect, rational, universally applicable moral solutions. Those following in the footsteps of Kant would undoubtedly bemoan the lack of a readily arrived at answer. After all, a fully rational ethics must be helpful. In order to be helpful it must provide guidance. To provide guidance, a nice fixed formula is immensely useful. It may not make for interesting literature, but it does make for clear moral directives.

Our take is somewhat different. Hospitality is important to philosophy, we argue, precisely because it makes demands yet does not follow a set of easy algorithms that generate infallible resolutions. Moral action still calls for guidance. Now, however, it comes in the form of regulative principles rather than absolute maxims. Such principles require attention to context, to the personalities of those involved, to time. Whereas much of traditional philosophy sought to remove the burden of responsibility from the individual, the mandate of hospitality highlights the unavoidable dimension of personal decision and commitment. Such considerations go a long way towards explaining why philosophers have discounted hospitality as a moral virtue and food as an important topic. As we have seen, food and hospitality do not lend themselves to formulas. Fortunately, poets and playwrights, closer to ordinary life and more comfortable with muddles, ambiguities and contradictions, have not discounted their value. Our thinking owes a lot to them.

Hospitality, Food and the Whole Human Being

The chief medium of hospitality is food. The work *Origins: A Short Etymological Dictionary of Modern English* by Eric Partridge suggests that the root *hos-* has, as its basic meaning, 'food (with shelter) as a means of preservation'. Certainly Baucis and Philemon understood hospitality as providing food – even at enormous cost to their own future comfort. Ovid's story, as well as Dante's, both of which emphasize hospitality as a serious obligation, seem far removed from present conceptions that emphasize the hospitality industry or hospitality as the entertaining of friends. Such marginalization of hospitality goes hand in hand with philosophy's marginalization of food. When philosophers do not take the table seriously, hospitality will not make it onto their lists of privileged virtues.

Philosophers must re-examine our older guiding ideas, especially those that insist on perfectly rational this and perfectly systematic that. Food – and our relations to and with it – provides powerful tools with which to undertake this re-examination. When we make the seemingly simple step of paying serious attention to the (unavoidable) fact that living beings need food, we actually effect dramatic changes in the way in which we do ethics.

For instance, by taking seriously our stomach-endowed identities, we swap the demand that humans be *rational* with the goal that we be *reasonable*. The older opposition, 'either rational or irrational', just does not capture the complications of the human condition. We are not just minds accidentally attached to bodies. Paying attention to our hungers and the modes via which we satisfy them will help us restore a fuller understanding of ourselves. It will move us beyond the position that made a fetish out of pure rationality, a position which arose out of the self-understanding built from the division of the human into mind and body. To make this fundamental philosophical shift it is necessary to alter a major idea that has dominated philosophy for a long time. It goes by the name of the mind–body dualism. It is credited to Descartes and was caricatured by Gilbert Ryle (1900–1976) as the 'ghost in the machine': the idea that humans are essentially immaterial minds that are somehow attached to material bodies.

A Guiding Idea that has Worn Out its Welcome

During the modern era of philosophy (a period roughly extending from the Renaissance to the First World War), the concrete, flesh-and-blood creatures who engaged in fleshy, emotional, reflective dealings with their surroundings were replaced by 'thinkers' who disconnected the mental side of human life from the physiological and social. ('Thinker' became a significant new synonym for 'philosopher'.) 'Man' (the gender-specific term is important) came to be considered as essentially 'mind'. The modern framework also occasioned new descriptive concepts. The flesh-and-blood human disappeared and was replaced by the 'rational animal' or 'rational agent'.

These were new concepts, new ways of encapsulating the motivating idea. Given the complexity of the human constitution, the idea of dualism was worth experimenting with. Philosophers asked how helpful it might be if we were to think of humans as combinations of two distinct and ultimately irreconcilable components, mind and body. Immediately, though, 'and' was transformed into 'versus' in the relationship between mind *and* body. In the rush to privilege the mind, the tendency was to highlight how utterly unlike the body it was. Once that step was taken, it was almost inevitable that a sharp opposition would be set up. Mind *versus* body contrasted the 'rational' side – that is, the properly and purely human side – with the 'non-rational', which easily morphed into the 'irrational' side. Whatever was not mind could only be other than purely human, a distraction that took us away from our more authentic, essential selves. The stomach and the food it needed were bound to fare badly within such a scheme.

Philosophers, being philosophers, got a lot of mileage out of the 'ghost in the machine' approach. That mileage was boosted by the kinds of examples and exemplary figures that philosophers chose to represent mind and rational behaviour. They tended, for instance, to focus on the figure of the geometer. Here is someone who, armed with axioms and logic, can arrive at answers using the mind alone. Given the measurements of two angles in a triangle, what is the third angle? The geometer can work this out with precision. Not only that, but the geometer can do so without even bothering to get out a compass and take actual measurements; indeed, actual measurements would just get in the way of the pristine perfection of ideal triangles. So prominent was the tug of geometry as a model approach that the Dutch philosopher Baruch

Spinoza (1632–1677) entitled his work on moral philosophy *Ethics, Demonstrated in Geometrical Order*, and constructed it in the style of geometry proofs.

Outside the model of geometry, it wasn't quite so easy to compartmentalize human activity into rational mind and irrational body. The generative idea of dualism always had trouble with emotions, feelings and appetites. These, after all, are central to a fully human life. But on the older mind–body framework, these were purely *bodily* activities – or were they? This was part of their trouble; they seemed to also have some powerful control over our rational selves – our minds. Emotions have often been identified as 'passions', a word that associates them solely with the body and suggests that they overwhelm the real self. 'We', it is assumed, are separate from our passions. A sharp incompatibility is thus set up between passions and what is claimed to be 'rational' thought. Appetites – for food, but also for sex and, more remotely, for possessions – similarly have been seen to 'take control' and render us incapable of clear thinking. Whether they were defined as bodily or mental, these dimensions of human life refused to go away quietly, as the police in the mind–body regime would have preferred.

Here we can begin to grasp the important work philosophy can do. In the mind–body dichotomy, a particular idea began to take hold and expand. Along with it came some new concepts ('rational animal', 'pure mind'), new shorthand ways of bringing together the diversity of experiences that always mark our situation. The generative idea and the concepts provide an orientation for dealing with our surroundings. The idea has taken hold because it gets at something important about life. At the same time, as its career develops, it tends to become more and more one-sided. What it leaves out (and focal ideas are always selective) comes back in the form of various conceptual and practical messes.

If we begin to see ourselves as minds attached to bodies, we will identify ourselves as 'rational agents'. Our bodies will be 'accidental' or non-essential features of our human being. Our emotions will come to be problems to be solved or reasoned away.

And – significant for our purposes here – competing models for ethics will hop back and forth between those that emphasize (pure, objective, universal) reason and those that emphasize ('impure', subjective, localized) 'feeling'. Hospitality, if it appears in such systems at all, would appear as a mere nicety, unconnected to any of the important ethical virtues like goodness, pity or justice.

This dismissal of something so crucial cannot be carried out forever. There are just too many dimensions of our lives tied to the stomach and the practices that accompany it. By *re*capturing something important about ourselves – namely, that we are stomach-endowed creatures – we can move to newer generative ideas. These in turn will retool the relationship between hospitality and ethics. When we 're-member' our stomachs, it is hard to feel like a ghost. But under the regime of mind–body thinking, considerations regarding food will always be relegated to the periphery, or will be wrestled into submission by ways of speaking that emphasize rationality. Food history in the United States gives us a good example of what can happen when such thinking dominates.

Rational Cooking and the Guest–Host Dynamic

Donna Gabaccia's *We Are What We Eat: Ethnic Food and the Making of Americans* (1998), a history of food practices in the United States, describes the situation well. It also provides a good example of the integral links between food and hospitality – and an illustration of why it is so important to take those links seriously. Nineteenth-century immigrants were introduced by their new American hosts to a universal, rational, 'scientific' standard of cookery, via the emerging field of domestic science, or home economics.[8] Fannie Farmer, a pioneer in this field, was known as the 'mother of level measurement', because her cookbook introduced the idea of using standardized measuring cups and spoons, replacing the more idiosyncratic and casual style of measurement that prevailed in earlier cookbooks. Surely a good idea, right? After all, if your teaspoon is three times bigger than mine, your teaspoon's worth of baking soda is going to have a dramatically different effect on your cake than mine. 'Straightening out' and standardizing recipe writing was seen as an aid to an increasingly mobile society in which young women might not be near enough to their mothers to ask them for advice on how to make their cakes rise properly.

But, as happens when burgeoning ideas take hold, the move to 'rationalize' the practices of the kitchen and dining room extended its reach far beyond the measuring spoon drawer. Such thinking was also deployed to straighten out the defective food habits that immigrants brought with them, replacing them with good old austere, New England cooking. Why New England cooking? Put simply, because New England was home to the country's (white) intellectual elite – and therefore was considered to be the home of the most 'rational' cookery in the nation. Immigrants were instructed to drink lots of milk and urged to move away from foods such as spaghetti or garlic.[9] 'Educated American women instead proposed to Americanize the foreigners, by teaching them what, and how, to eat, and by developing a "domestic science" or "home economics" appropriate for American citizens.'[10] 'Rational cooking' would replace the purportedly helter-skelter approach used by immigrant families.[11] While the domestic science movement insisted on a rational transformation of immigrant cookery, it is clear that ethnocentric suspicion was at the real heart of much of the reform. Ingredients strongly associated with immigrants, like garlic, were among those most targeted for elimination. After all, Uncle Sam did not want to be 'swallowed by foreigners' (and with bad breath, at that).[12] So much for hospitality.

Admittedly, the recommendations of the domestic science movement were not completely without flair. As immigrants moved into the middle class, they were expected to share in 'the pleasures of preparing and serving all-white or all-pink meals'.[13] If ever there was a mess calling for important philosophical reconstruction, meals of 'all-pink' or 'all-white' foods would likely be right up there. Now that this point has been reached, it is time to take a good look at the cluster of assumptions that brought us to such a pass.

In terms of our initial 'mess' – the quandary about whether it is the host or the guest who is responsible for making accommodations – Gabaccia's text establishes one clear answer. In the era of the 'rational cookery' movement, it was the strangers, the immigrants, the guests who had to adapt. Hosts – that is, the European Americans who had been immigrants a generation or two earlier and who now were established as 'real Americans' – set and imposed standards, and even policed them. The Nobel Peace Prize winner Jane Addams (1860–1935), the progressive founder of Hull House in Chicago, a settlement community grounded in the idea that new immigrants are wise, knowledgeable new members of the community who have important contributions to make to the fabric of the nation, even fell into the line of thinking that saw immigrant diets as something in need of reform.

All of this made perfect sense in a context explicitly and implicitly shaped by the idea that rational 'ghosts' (a role played here by members of the intellectual elite centred in Boston) rightly impose rules on the bodily 'machine' (with which 'backward', ill-educated immigrants were associated). But prescriptions for 'all-white' meals, along with immigrants' sense of the value of their own cuisines, occasioned questioning on all sides. For the immigrants, questioning drew upon a desire to retain their old world practices ('keep your milk: wine and coffee worked fine for my ancestors and they will do just as well for me'). Others chafed at the austere, plain foods promoted by 'rational' cooking. No garlic? Or, for that matter, no flavouring beyond salt and – for the bold – a bit of pepper? Finally, where would we place our faith in humanity if no one balked at the promise of all-pink or all-white meals as our outlets for 'creativity'? For philosophers, questions such as these call us to examine the guiding ideas that gave rise to such messy situations in the first place.

Dualism, the older idea which made a sharp mind–body separation, simply ignored too much of the nitty-gritty in human life; as such it was built on a distorted picture of the human condition. Taking food seriously means treating humans as flesh-and-blood creatures, not as 'rational agents'. Such a move should not be all that unusual, but philosophical plumbing, we recall, changes slowly.

Ethics is Hospitality

Not surprisingly, those at the forefront of re-examining and rearranging the ideas that dominated the modern European heritage traced their roots to traditions other than those of modernity. As mentioned briefly earlier, literature was one area that, unlike philosophy, gave a privileged place to hospitality. Another source in which hospitality is taken seriously is the heritage of religions. In the West, leading figures who have rethought ethics in ways that draw from hospitality (or something akin to it) make connections to cultural memories of being wanderers without a home that have been preserved in the Hebrew Bible and Jewish traditions.

The French moral thinker Emmanuel Levinas (1906–1995) was the first such figure. In several profound and challenging texts,[14] Levinas circumvented both the philosophical activity that prizes mind as the central orientation for philosophy (epistemology) and that which prizes being (metaphysics) – two strands of philosophy that have predominated in the modern West. Instead, he argued, the proper central orientation for philosophy is ethics. Such an ethics he envisioned in concrete terms, modelled on face-to-face relationships, focusing especially on relationships with those defined as the 'other'. Such a shift from metaphysics and epistemology to ethics led Levinas, in turn, to re-valorize hospitality. Ethics and hospitality, rather than occupying separate realms, came to be understood in terms of each other. Unlike the kind of hospitality that in practice means 'invite only people like us', Levinas' other is genuinely other, different from 'us' (whoever we are) in significant, unavoidable ways.

Inspired by Levinas, Jacques Derrida (1930–2004) proclaimed dramatically that ethics *is* hospitality. This is because ethics is concerned with the way we inhabit our world, and hospitality is the activity that can best serve to guide humans in properly inhabiting the world that is our home. The host–guest relationship becomes the paradigm, the model for typifying how our search for living a good life plays itself out.

Henri Bergson (1859–1941), another French philosopher rooted in the Hebrew tradition, had earlier distinguished between an 'open' and a 'closed' morality, concepts that also draw upon something like hospitality for their meaning.[15] A closed morality can be envisioned as a walled-in city. The primary response to outsiders: suspicion and rejection. A contemporary example illustrates Bergson's meaning. In her *Day of Honey: A Memoir of Food, Love, and War* (2011), the American reporter Annia Ciezadlo relates a story about the former Iraqi dictator Saddam Hussein. He consolidated power by closing Iraq off from the rest of the world: '"Teach the child to beware of the foreigner," he instructed in a speech . . . Giving your business or even your child a foreign name was suspect. Meeting a "foreigner" was enough to get you interrogated.'[16] Open morality, on the other hand, signifies a kind of humble willingness not just to welcome those who are different, but also to regard such meetings as opportunities for growth and development. The shift aims one's concern for the good (a quintessential concern of ethics in the West) in the direction of guest–host relations. It opens up, simultaneously, a novel pathway for philosophy.

From Geometer to Farmer

As we have seen, the focal idea of dualism brought with it the representative figure of the geometer. A model centred on stomach-endowed selves and associated with hospitality, however, calls for a different representative figure. The geometer won't do. Prototypes of hospitality cannot carry out their work entirely within their own minds, calling on nothing but reason. Hospitable types cannot rely entirely on their 'minds' – their powers of rationality – to address the needs of their guests. Hosts who do not think from and with their bodily being will be unable to get in touch with the needs of their guests.

The food world of course abounds with people in the 'hospitality industry' – people whose jobs it is to 'see to the comfort' of others. While we might well find many representative figures from within that industry, we point instead to a somewhat more unlikely figure: the farmer. And we begin our analysis of the farmer with perhaps the most dramatic story of farmer hospitality imaginable: Phocas, the Christian patron saint of gardening, the man who composted himself.

According to William Bryant Logan's book *Dirt: The Ecstatic Skin of the Earth* (1995), Phocas was a late first-century (others suggest third-century) Christian peasant living in Sinope, a town on a peninsula in the Black Sea. When Roman soldiers were sent there to dispatch him, Phocas actually offered the soldiers lodging. They had come to his house asking for the whereabouts of Phocas, not realizing that they were looking at him. The soldiers enjoyed his bed and board. After they went to sleep, Phocas headed for his garden to dig a large hole, of sufficient size to easily fit the body of a headless man. In the morning, after he had served them a hearty breakfast, Phocas told the soldiers, 'I'm your man', and obligingly went out into the garden to let them chop off his head. Logan likes to imagine the perplexed soldiers, grateful that their target had obliged them so courageously,

> carefully covering the hole with soil . . . It was the least
> they could do for a man who'd taken such good care of
> them. And we must imagine the thoroughness of Phocas's
> simple and hospitable soul, which took such care to return
> to the garden the body that had taken sustenance from it.[17]

Farmers grow food in and through a world that is unavoidably, essentially made up of soil, sun, rain, insects, animals and plants, not to mention other people, and institutions such as the economy and the government. Not all of these features of the world of which they are a part are equally conducive to the growing of that food. No matter; these are the components of the world, and it will not do to 'bracket' them the way a geometer can bracket the imperfect triangles of the paper world. Nor will it do to say 'it's all subjective', a line of thought fairly laughable for the farmer. The point of departure for the farmer prototype is no longer a mind confronting 'external' objects, but something more primordial: humans dealing with their surroundings and attempting to do so in optimally 'good' ways – that is, ethically. Mental triangles may indeed be better (in the sense of more given to purity and certitude) than material ones, but mental food just isn't better than material food.

Another reason the farmer is an apt replacement for the geometer has to do with farmers' relationships with the soil itself – with dirt. Logan writes,

> Hospitality is the fundamental virtue of the soil. It makes room. It shares. It neutralizes poisons. And so it heals. This is what the soil teaches: If you want to be remembered, give yourself away.[18]

We would add that the soil also teaches that, if you want to be a good guest, you must be sure to give your host something in return. The Latin word *hospes* means both guest and host, signalling the reciprocal and porous nature of the relationship between the two (a subject to which we will return later). The soil illustrates this powerfully, by nourishing the plants upon which humans rely for sustenance. But when soil itself is not given sustenance – when humans do not play 'host' to it – its capacity to nourish life can be severely depleted.

Taking the farmer as a representative figure alters our philosophical plumbing system in important ways.[19] First of all, we humans are recognized and appreciated in our concrete fullness. No longer can we be reduced to 'rational agents'. Terms to describe this concrete fullness are hard to come by; all of them seem to retain the notion of mind-in-body. What we seek are terms that acknowledge, as the American philosopher John Dewey (1859–1952) suggested, that 'mindedness' is more a particular evolutionary feature of certain kinds of bodily beings than it is a 'thing' riding around inside of those bodies.

Second, farmers are dependent on a number of factors not of their own making. In a sense farmers are guests drawing on the bounty supplied by the host. Admittedly the host – that is, the earth – could have arranged things a little better, making the work of growing food less onerous, but the fact remains that humans are, in many ways, like guests making use of and drawing on what the host has supplied.

A related, third, alteration has to do with the contingent, alternating nature of guest and host. As we noted earlier, the Latin word *hospes* means both guest and host, as the French term *hôte* still does today. Anthropology teaches that most, if not all, of us have our origins somewhere else in the world. The person we identify as a homebody and host is simply someone who has, for a while, paused their wandering. Employment relocation, desire for a different climate, the wish to live with a loved one, might set one to wandering once again. Such reasons can be complemented by more troubling ones: natural disasters, economic crises, wars or ecological catastrophes. To acknowledge that we all are – or could easily become – wanderers again is one of the powerful features of this word in its Latin and French forms. An ethics grounded in this acknowledgement will recognize the importance of generosity offered to the wandering stranger; of hospitality. It will, more generally, recognize that ethics is all about the kind of home we are willing to make.

A fourth alteration also relates to the ambiguous meaning of *hospes* as both host and guest. This ambiguity helps bring to light how it is the relationship rather than the separate units that is central. Within the 'rational agent' take on things, there are 'subjects' (essentially, minds receiving data) and, elsewhere, 'objects' (essentially, data to be received and worked on by the mind). *Hospes* disallows such a neat separation. The term identifies complementary positions within a relationship, positions that can alter. Counterintuitive as it may seem, if anything is primary, it is the relationship.

Replacing subject and object with guest and host suggests a final important alteration in our intellectual plumbing. The 'rational agent', thinking of geometrical puzzles as the ideal, can imagine that all enigmatic situations are resolvable by resorting to Kantian-style maxims for definitive, incontrovertible, clearly evident resolutions. For several centuries such certitude, no matter how foreign to the actual experiences had by parents, friends, stock traders, political leaders, diplomats or judges, maintained a stubborn hold as a goal to be attained. As the twentieth century dawned, critics of modern philosophy began to question this ideal.[20] Truths, not certitudes, became the proper goals of inquiries.

Within this different take on things, critical questions about the modern philosophical inheritance come to the fore. Why assume that oversimplified situations should be the rule or paradigm, rather than the exception? Why translate the complexities of existence so that they fit neatly into some preferred grid that privileges certitude over truth? Why move from experience-based food-making to 'scientific' or 'rational' cooking? Why draw a sharp boundary between hospitality and ethics? Such questions send us back, once again, to literature.

Stomach-endowed Philosophy Welcomes Literature

Commensality, the sophisticated way of saying 'eating together', has traditionally been a hallmark of hospitality. Odysseus, archetypal wanderer-outsider-stranger, asks a key question when he arrives in a new land: 'Are there bread eaters here?' Robert Fagles renders it as 'men like us perhaps, who live on bread?'[21] 'Are there bread eaters here?' is actually shorthand; the fuller formula is the oft-repeated enquiry concerning inhabitants about to be encountered: are they hospitable? 'What *are* they here? – violent, savage, lawless? or friendly to strangers, god-fearing men?'[22] Slightly amended, the key formulation could then become: 'are there bread *sharers* here?' Homer makes clear that a fully humane life is marked by how one welcomes guests. Such a welcome always involves food. Each book of his *Odyssey* includes some manifestation of behaviour which either models or distorts hospitality.

Homer's other famed epic poem, the *Iliad*, offers a proto-typical, oft-cited scene. It involves two warriors. Diomedes is a fierce fighter for the Greeks, a kind of unstoppable killing machine. Glaukos, a fearless soldier on the Trojan side, decides to engage Diomedes in combat. The latter, stunned, thinks at first that this is some god in disguise and thus a trap (for surely no mere mortal would be foolish enough to challenge him). He asks Glaukos about himself. The soldier replies that he is fully human, the grandson of Bellerophon. Immediately, Diomedes loses all belligerence. It turns out that his grandfather, Oineus, had once welcomed Bellerophon and hosted him for twenty days. These ties of hospitality automatically bind Diomedes and Glaukos, meaning that hostilities are ceased. They are honour-bound to repeat the hospitality of their ancestors.[23] As a sign of this reinvigorated bond they exchange armour.

The meeting could have turned out otherwise. When Diomedes first questions him, Glaukos wonders aloud why genealogy would be important. Dead ancestors are like leaves in autumn; newer generations are like buds in springtime. Disconnection, then fresh starts. Diomedes knows better. Entanglement is a precious creation. Dissolution, ruptures and their associated enmities are all too common. In life, the greater good goes to creation rather than destruction, to fostering attachments, not to encouraging estrangement, division and separation.

We are brought back here to the Derrida position: hospitality is ethics. Hospitality as a virtue urges us to combat complacency.

It motivates us to seek connections and, yes, entanglements. The Homeric emphasis on gift exchange adds an important, often overlooked, dimension. The provision of food as gift identifies one important move in mutual entanglement. In addition, guests themselves are like gifts. They bring something new and valuable by their very presence. So too do they bring complications, perhaps discomfort and certainly the need for patience. Not only is there opportunity for new connections, there is opportunity for personal growth. Additionally, as the recipient of a visit, now thought of as a gift, the host becomes indebted to the guest. That is why, among Homeric personages, it was the host who gave departing gifts to the guest. Both guest and host become indebted to each other.

This puts into play an important pattern involving gift exchanges. Gift exchanges form an important part of the hospitality ritual because they keep the entanglement active. Unlike economic or contractual arrangements, the mutual obligations associated with hospitality are ongoing. Merely contractual arrangements fit the pattern of Glaukos' autumn leaves falling from trees: each signee to a contract has agreed to provide some service or compensation, and once the service or compensation has been accomplished, the connection is no more. The sharing of meals and gifts, by contrast, is meant to be continual. Some imbalance is always present. The pattern: 'give, receive, give in return . . .' identifies an open-ended process. There can be no closure. The older ideal of ethical closure in a decision that is fixed, finished and final is set aside. Within the newer context, hospitality moves to the centre, and the 'point' of hospitality is not the discharge of its obligations. It is rather embeddedness in an unending process, the process of reworking our dwelling: namely, the process of organizing the activities associated with our home so that they are guided by the ideal of hospitality.

Problems with Homeric Hospitality

If guests are like gifts, who themselves receive gifts of food, then this exchange opens up a process where threads link individuals. Gratitude is manifested in action by how one gives in return. It is also manifested in terms of who qualifies as worthy recipients of this beneficence. At this point, the Homeric emphasis, impressive as it is, runs against some limitations. The difficulty emerges when we consider the matter of the stranger. Who are Homer's 'strangers'? Homer's characters, who live out an ethos of hospitality, resemble each other. Even Glaukos and Diomedes, though enemies, have much in common. Neither resembles a poor beggar, a slave or a 'foreigner'. Diomedes even suspects that Glaukos might be a god.

The welcome offered by ancient Greek hospitality is dependent upon pre-existing connections. These connections can result from having a common ancestor, from shared undertakings, from class solidarity, from a bond established in previous generations or from some combination of these. Such parameters point to a limitation with the conceptual plumbing of Homer's ideas. The general scheme of ideas in his community tilts in the direction of homogeneity. As praiseworthy as his attitude to the stranger is, the Homeric stance draws sharp lines of demarcation. In their own context, the lines are hardly noticed. The plumbing works so well for so many that it is assumed to work well for all. Or it is assumed that those for whom it does not work – those who are genuinely and deeply 'Other', by virtue of class or ethnicity or race – don't matter in the same ways. The impulse of hospitality does not extend to them. How do we make visible the existence of those for whom the plumbing *doesn't* work – those to whom hospitality is not, and never will be, extended in the Homeric context, those who lie beyond those charmed circles of contact that make connection possible?

Derrida re-enters at this point. He insists that we take seriously the otherness of the other. Only in doing so does one bring the full meaning of hospitality to fruition. He does this by pointing to a disparity between current conditions ('this is the way "we" do hospitality') and the prototype or ideal that serves as a lure for us ('but is there another way that is better?'). Derrida characterizes this disparity as a gap between the 'Law of hospitality' on one hand, and the 'laws of hospitality' on the other. His capital-L 'Law' is a universal mandate (in principle unrealizable) to offer hospitality to everyone always. The actual settings in which we find ourselves are represented by the plural, lower-case 'laws'.

Between the two is a yawning gap of insurmountable breadth. But lest it seem pointless and vicious to articulate this difference, note that, without the laws (read: actual laws as well as customs, habits, practices) of hospitality, the universal demand remains empty and impotent. And, without the universal Law, the local customs remain stagnant, ignorantly provincial and inadequate. The Law remains idealistic (read: meaningless) without the laws. The laws, without the Law, remain narrow, restricted and prone to devolve into sharp us/them distinctions.[24] The former ethics is open but hollow. The latter has concrete application but is closed, tending to self-satisfaction at best and xenophobia at worst. Blending concrete application and openness becomes the new guiding ideal. Just as homeowners continuously tinker and alter their physical abodes, so the ethical abode must also regularly be remodelled.

Taking the hospitality turn seriously, we can now see, makes a considerable difference. The initial ethical question shifts from the open-ended and individualized 'what should I do' to the more concrete and shared 'what kind of home are we making?' To answer this question we have to move again in the more concrete dimension and answer other questions: whom are we inviting to share our table? Are our tables cordoned off and turned in on themselves? Do walls or doors predominate in our homes; are they closed and guarded, or open and welcoming – and to whom? These are the fundamental questions that explain why hospitality *is* ethics.

The boundaries of good homes are porous. The Law of hospitality demands that they be completely so. But here, as anywhere, a good position pushed to an extreme turns not simply into an impossible one, but actually into an evil one. A complete porousness would eliminate any sense or meaning associated with one's 'home'. One would, in fact, have lost any opportunity to offer hospitality. The Greeks knew this, which is why they made a central virtue of achieving the proper balance. Today we translate this as 'moderation', but this word now has connotations of tepid, careful, compromising behaviour, connotations unreflective of the struggle necessary to achieve what is good in particular circumstances (which defined the older model).

The porousness of hospitality, while it can never be perfectly practised, also disallows any sense of comfort or self-satisfaction. The call remains insistent and inviolable. It is also primordial. In these ways, Derrida's call to universal hospitality differs sharply from the more typical demand that we welcome in the stranger. The Law/laws alternatives, one beginning with the closed home and the other with an open one, offer important contrasts. The closed scheme is turned around completely when the open one becomes primary. The more familiar closed scheme embodies a sort of 'concentric circles' approach: obligations start not with the call to universal hospitality, but with a sense of duty, initially to oneself, then, in expanding circles, to those varying in degrees of distance from us. This metaphor has a venerable history, going back as far as the Stoics.[25] Within the closed scheme, each move to a new, larger circle is understood as an expansion of generosity. Such an expansion model starts from a point of comfort: duty to oneself and loved ones. Beyond that, each move is one for which we can be congratulated. After all, it is selflessness and generosity that impel us forward. We can commend ourselves on our increasing levels of munificence as we move towards more distant rings (from self to family, then to friends, neighbours, community members, all humans, then to animals, plants and eventually the whole planet).

For those who start with the closed home and move through different layers of openness, there is an order of ever-increasing self-congratulation. The alternative we are promoting leaves less room for comfort. When we start with the open home, there are, by contrast, varying layers of guilt. There is a realization that the universal Law cannot possibly be met; we will always fall short. To make local hospitality real, and indeed possible, universal hospitality has to be limited. The universal Law thus makes central a feeling much maligned in our world: guilt. However, since 'guilt' is almost inexpugnably negative, inducing a form of self-laceration that actually limits our ability to act at all helpfully, it might be best to refer instead to 'shortcoming' or 'deficiency' of some sort. Such ideas emphasize motivation, especially motivation *to work for* conditions that maximize local hospitality.

Problems with Derridean Hospitality

All of this is well taken and goes some distance to correct the limitations of Homeric hospitality: the gap between the Law of hospitality and the laws of hospitality; the concrete inclusion of hospitality to fill in what 'good' can mean; the motivating force of the newer grasp of things. Still, Molière lurks in the background. Some outsiders *need* to be turned away. *Hostis*, the stranger, *can* be an enemy. We need to return here also to another ambiguity encapsulated in the related Latin term *hospes*. By meaning both host and guest, it implies that neither takes ultimate priority. Individuals may be hosts or guests depending on the circumstances. An important philosophical shift, as we have already discussed, involves paying attention to the relationship, not just to the individual terms. *Hostis* indicates a tension before it indicates one or the other of fixed meanings it can take. *Hospes* also indicates a tension prior to assuming a fixed meaning.

Derrida is helpful in indicating the reciprocating back-and-forth between the Law and the laws of hospitality. The advantage derives from what emerges: there is nothing more basic than the tension between them. Strange as it may seem to us who still live within the intellectual landscape of modernity, there is no going beyond the tensional interplay to a single foundation that underlies it all and renders it harmonious. In Derrida's spirit, we would call for the need to recognize other basic tensions. For instance, no automatic label accompanies unknown visitors. They could be strangers in need or enemies intent on harm. The fundamental nature of this tension ('potential friend or potential foe?') helps indicate why Kantian dreams of fixed, certain answers, though always tempting, are misguided. When no single element is basic, when tension among components is primary, the need for prudent choices will always be present (which is not to say that such choices will always be possible; sometimes the enemy is discovered too late, and sometimes the potential friend is turned away too soon). Not only does the Law of hospitality have to be tempered for practical reasons (the house is full, the budget limited), it has to be tempered because it does not always lead to good results. Discernment and selectivity can hardly be avoided in concrete situations involving actual humans.

Farmers, who work within natural and thus somewhat unpredictable conditions, have no problem recognizing that they are always called upon to take responsibility for acts of discernment. Do we harvest this week, hoping that there will be no frost, or next week, when the fruit will be sweeter? Evidence, experience and experts can help. But no algorithmic formula will generate a fixed, error-proof response. Some risk–responsibility dimension always remains. Philosophers, though, following some traditional models, tend to flee responsibility. The Kant-inspired thinker seeks refuge in universal maxims. The sceptic asserts that 'there are no standards', 'it's all subjective'. Both agree on one point: the tough work of achieving the right response in these particular circumstances can be short-circuited. When ethics is hospitality no such short-cut, no such oversimplification, is possible. The universal demand is recognized. The need for personal responsibility is recognized. The farmer offers a better model than the geometer.

Back to the Beginning

The philosophical term for taking on this kind of responsibility is 'prudential judgement'. Just as farmers depend on experience, on science, on advice from friends, so prudential judgements are best arrived at by thoughtful, reasonable considerations. Reasonable considerations themselves become more justifiable as they are shaped by a cluster of guiding procedures. In the case of hospitality, a six-part pattern for appraisal moves to the centre of our lives as ethical beings:

1) A 'good' life is one that is open and hospitable.
2) Hospitality, like any virtue, can be perverted if it is turned into an idol demanding uncritical worship.
3) Because of this danger, prudential judgement based on evidence and experience – what Aristotle called *phronesis* – will always, and should always, be part of the mix.
4) In making decisions, it is important to think in terms of prototypical cases that lie on either end of a spectrum and offer relatively little controversy. We can then work towards the middle, asking for the appropriate analogies. To which end of the spectrum does the present difficult case most belong? Why do we think so?
5) In addition to cases, it is important to identify representative individuals who present models of the kind of behaviour that is sought. A good life then becomes one that follows the right models, rather than one that deduces the proper behaviour from fixed rules.
6) All situations must be subjected to a threshold test. Given the likelihood that borderline cases will provide the greatest difficulties, alternative possibilities must be examined in terms of whether they are within or surpass a particular threshold. At which point

would reasonable accommodations pass over into unreasonable, overly restrictive ones?

We can now return to the quandary with which we opened this chapter. Is it the locavore guest who must adapt to the food laid out by the hostess? Is it the hostess who should have enquired about her guests' preferences and adapted her menu? With whom does responsibility lie?

To begin with, the general principle that we ought to be hospitable puts us into the proper setting, but is not all that helpful. The specific question has to do with what behaviours best serve proper hospitality. Since the hospitality setting immediately implicates both guests and hosts, we have a positive opening orientation. Hospitality brings with it responsibilities for *both* host and guest. Again, this does not take us very far but keeps us on a path that can bring resolution. It at least means that the real question is not which of the two, the guest or the host, should bend and accommodate the other; that very question presumes a distinction we are challenging, and would shape a particular answer. Our alternative account suggests that the answer to the question 'who should accommodate whom?' is, 'It depends.'

To move further towards a resolution, we bring into play some other elements in our pattern for appraisal. Working from the ends of a spectrum towards the middle can often be helpful. At one (minimally controversial) end, we find the host-accommodating prototype: guests suffer from allergies that make them seriously ill and perhaps threaten their lives; as such, the host could cause major harm, which can readily be avoided by adjusting the menu. At the other minimally controversial end we find the guest-accommodating prototype: some guests are locavores; the host is on a very limited budget. There are many considerations in play at the dinner: friendship, sociability, perhaps a host returning a favour, congeniality, not wanting to hurt someone's feelings and a commitment to locavore practices. In a case like this one, to insist that one's commitments to the ingredients' source automatically trump the other considerations – especially when this would place a special financial burden on the host – would appear to tilt towards vice rather than virtue.

Then there are the borderline cases. What if only one person is committed to vegetarianism, or the South Beach diet? Towards which prototypical end do these situations tend? Should these predilections mean that the host must alter plans to present a dish for which she has spent several months planning? Probably not, but only if some accommodation can be made for the vegetarian or Beach guest, who in turn must accommodate and adjust to the food served. Should the threshold test suggest that, after a certain point of accommodation, the host's plan for an exercise in creative artistry or nutritionally balanced meal, or both, will be disrupted, then the level of adjustment should stop short of that moment.

Hospes and *hostis* are irredeemably fuzzy terms, depicting undeniably fuzzy relationships; the stranger–enemy tension in one case, the host/guest ambiguity in the other. Within such a context, practical prudential decisions are the best we have. Within the hospitality-is-ethics template there is no ultimate single formula via which we can escape from the risk and anxiety of responsibility. Nor is there the easy escape into the realm of scepticism, the other strategy for evading the anxiety of responsibility. At the root of things lies neither some version of a fixed geometrical figure, nor just jumbled, neutral stuff. Instead, in *hospes/hostis* there is a vibrant, living, resonating tension.

A Nobel Prize-winning Exemplar

Within the guest–host paradigm, personal considerations take on an integral role alongside the guiding ideals. Within the six-part pattern of appraisal outlined above, personal considerations emerge in several ways, one of which is the identification of admirable, and thus model, individuals. Whereas Kantian ethics (to continue the example of an ethical system grounded in rule-following) focuses on the way in which individual actions adhere to abstract codes, the hospitality model focuses on how individuals live out 'focal valuations' – that is, the principles deemed to be most worthy for living good lives. These individuals living in a context that privileges focal evaluations become the 'inspirational individuals' whose lives serve as exemplars. Note that the exemplars can be of good or ill; they can indicate a trajectory to be avoided as well as one to be emulated. What counts is how we situate ourselves in relation to them, how we decide where the analogies lie between our behaviours and theirs. Inspirational individuals may be real or fictional. In light of how important having a figure who can embody hospitality is to the undertaking that privileges food and hospitality, we end with a real inspirational figure whose trajectory centres on hospitality.

A philosophy recognizing the importance of the stomach and of hospitality cannot remain a philosophy committed simply to abstract principles. For guidance in actual circumstances it is important to be able to situate ourselves within certain kinds of narratives and attempt to figure out what model figures would have done. Our model figure, Jane Addams (mentioned earlier in relation to immigrant meals in the United States), was the first American woman to receive the Nobel Peace Prize. She, along with Homer, represent touchstone narratives for us. Furthermore, her narrative provides the needed cosmopolitan corrective to Homer's closed system of hospitality. His stories present us with fictional accounts. Addams's is a story of a real individual. Neighbourliness was her watchword. In no way could she be described as an outside spectator, though that could easily have been the path she took. She was born in a well-off family, the kind of family that, in late nineteenth-century America, believed in educating women. Such an education, which usually included a year spent in Europe, was meant to 'refine' young ladies, not lead them to pursue lives of social action – genteel concern from a distance, maybe, but not direct participation. In other words, in most ways, Jane Addams was a prototype of the upper-middle-class, white, Protestant, well-rooted American.

Late nineteenth-century America was also the new home to a very ethnically diverse group of individuals who had come to the United States from south and central Europe. These newcomers could not have been more unlike the family of Jane Addams: neither genteel nor middle class, they were mostly poor and very often illiterate. Instead of refined liberal Protestantism, the immigrants brought traditions with them that most Americans would have seen as barbarous: superstitious versions of Christianity, mostly Catholicism, but also Greek and Russian Orthodoxy, along with the religion against which Christianity often defined itself – Judaism. Some of the immigrants, such as the Italians and the Irish, were not considered fully 'white'. Crowded into big cities, they led difficult and rough lives. Chicago, the city Jane Addams would make her home, was described as 'first in violence, deepest in dirt; loud, lawless, unlovely, ill-smelling, new; an overgrown gawk of a village, the teeming tough among cities. Criminally, it was wide open; commercially, it was brazen; and socially it was thoughtless and raw.'[26] Looked at from the perspective of the genteel middle class, it would have been easy to do little but complain about the newcomers. They could be described as ignorant, violent, backward, superstitious, incompetent, alcohol-drenched, not to mention prone to having lots of children – children whose main trajectory in life would be that of delinquency.

Jane Addams stands as an aspirational individual for us because this it not how she saw the new immigrants. She and some associates who were similarly socially situated decided to *become neighbours* to them. Doing so required a conscious, specifically planned action. They moved into a neighbourhood that was dirty, lawless, loud and smelly. Although themselves well-established residents of the United States, it is they who would, in their new surroundings, be the strangers, the outsiders, the guests. At the same time, as part of the privileged elite, their role would also be that of hosts.

The establishment founded by Addams was the first American example of the new 'settlement houses' that had begun in

London. 'Hull House', as she named it, would serve as a home for Addams and her companions in the midst of the newcomers' neighbourhood. At the same time it would serve as a gathering place for newly arrived immigrants, a site in which they could undertake the work of transition and translation. Hull House would ease the adjustment to their new homeland by teaching them English, assisting with work and housing, and guiding them through the maze of city services. It would assist newcomers in translating themselves to each other and to the guiding principles of their new land. Addams and her associates would live out the ambiguity of *hospes*; they would be both guests and hosts. They would try to live out the ambiguity of the one and the many, inculcating the principles of a democratic republic, while encouraging continuities with the traditional ways of the newcomers.

Why take on this unavoidably fraught role of guest and host in such a challenging context? Why go out of one's way to be neighbourly and hospitable – *and* to make oneself a stranger? Addams provided many reasons to do so: the allure of realizing democracy's ideals, a natural impulse to help others, a religious tradition of humanitarianism, a philosophical outlook that assumes the solidarity of the human race, a sense of justice characterized by broadened sympathies and a recognition of how social relations are inherently reciprocal.[27] Underlying all of this reasoning is a rejection of the spectator understanding of human life, the notion that 'we are really just minds'. Addams desired 'to live in a really living world and refus[ed] to be content with a shadowy intellectual or aesthetic reflection of it.'[28] She described her adventure as one in which she 'was launched deep into the stormy intercourse of human life', pointing out that when a 'mind is pliant under the pressure of events and experiences, it becomes hard to detach it' from the bodied-ness of such experiences.[29] It might have been hard for someone like Addams to detach mind from body, but not, as we have seen, for some philosophers, who actually developed, cultivated and prized the detached attitude, indeed, made it a generative idea.

With Addams, we find ourselves in the presence of some-one who does not take on the role of indifferent disembodied 'subject' confronting a discreet, separate 'object' as the natural starting point for human experience. Rather, she acknowledged that we are already and always within the 'stormy intercourse of human life'. Within that storm we can stake out various pos-itions, grounded in any of a number of virtues. Many of them are good. Tolerance, charity, prudence, justice and patience are worth prizing. Addams stands out for us because, among the cluster of virtues that define a good life, she chose hospitality as the overarching one. For the ethical question 'yes, but is it good?', an Addams-inspired, more concrete synonym would be, 'yes, but is it neighbourly?'

When hospitality becomes a model virtue, certain things follow in its wake. Clusters – and the tensions among them – replace the binary oppositions of the earlier either/or philosophies. Tensions are never solved by opting for one or other term. Rather, what we call *thoughtful practice* – what Addams preferred to call a 'thesis supported by experience'[30] – offers the best approach. In addition, difference is recognized in both its positive and negative dimensions. The people in whose neighbourhood Jane Addams lived could hardly be more different from the young people with whom she grew up, went to school or accompanied on European journeys. Yet, so prominent was the compulsion to live out what Derrida called the Law of hospitality that she and her colleagues went out of their way to associate with, learn from and provide a welcome for these 'others', outsiders to the United States, but insiders in the neighbourhood enclave to which she moved.

In choosing to live in a community with new immigrants, Addams and her associates kept alive the sense of reciprocal dependence (a version of what we have called 'resonating tension'), which was a key assumption underlying their work. Reciprocal dependence immediately blocks the tendency to phrase things as dilemmas which emphasize either/or; they cannot be treated as incompatible logical contradictories. Instead, tensions have to be dealt with and lived with by inventing reasonable accommodations. Reasonable accommodations do not have clean, sharp edges; they do not involve tidy breaks with the past. Instead, they are the work of massaging, finessing and easing incompatible positions into some kind of accord. The results may not feel very dramatic.

Should the newcomers assimilate or should they be treated with multicultural 'tolerance'? For the friends of scientific cooking, as we have seen, the answer was simple. The immigrants had to abandon their old ways: there was a new, scientific, progressive dietary model, and that was the one to follow. For twentieth-century multiculturalists, by contrast, each group had to have its identity acknowledged and preserved. Regarded as a purely logical dilemma (something it is not difficult to do), one horn or the other had to be chosen.

Addams saw things in a more complicated way. Her take was more in line with what we have identified as 'reasonable accommodation', arrived at via 'thoughtful practice': 'One thing seemed clear in regard to entertaining immigrants; to preserve and keep whatever of value their past life contained and to bring them in contact with a better type of Americans.'[31] Addams admitted and embraced the observation that her work was an 'experimental effort'. The combat of ideas arranged into a logical dilemma might be attractive to those who love puzzles and paradoxes. But clear, neat incompatibility, although possible to fabricate in the world of abstractions, has little place in the nitty gritty of an actual neighbourhood. Indeed, the one possibility she most dreaded was that her project would 'lose its flexibility, its power of quick adaptation, its readiness to change its methods as its environment may demand'.[32] Perfection, certitude and ideological purity were out of the question. Goodness, justice and truth, though, were always front and centre. No doubt the balancing act did not always come off as well as it could have. No doubt either that the flexible, experimental balancing act was exactly what should have been attempted.

The 'ethics is hospitality' approach will be messier and less definitive than the more logically rigorous one. It will result in a less-than-clear answer to the question 'what should we do?' Indeed, it transforms that question into one that asks 'what kind of home should we make?' It does not overlook the flesh-and-blood setting within which difficulties must be resolved. It is rooted in a creative and ever-present tension: that between the Law of Universal Hospitality and the laws of hospitality. This tension – and here we sound a theme that will become familiar to readers – is neither a problem to be solved nor a battle in which one combatant must be vanquished. We must, with Addams, resist reducing life's complications to 'logical dogmas'.[33] Instead, when we face real, irreducible clusters of elements in tension, we seek thoughtful resolutions. When successful, such thoughtful practice helps work through the very real tensions that result when sharply different groups have to live side by side. When hospitality is ethics, actual human models become our guides. In this sense, Jane Addams, with her sense of broadened sympathies, her emphasis on neighbourliness, her attempt to help people better get along with each other, is surely paradigmatic.

II

Food as/and Art

Aesthetic Eating

The country: Spain. The region: Catalonia. The city: Girona. The place: El Celler, an ultra-chic restaurant. The event: food journalist Adam Gopnik is presented with a dessert, an item the chef describes as still in the trial stages. The 'actual' dessert – the edible portion, that is – consists of three meringues and a white chocolate ball. But the dessert *experience* is something else altogether. The event is highly scripted, even including sound: an MP3 recording of Barcelona football club player Lionel Messi scoring a goal. The three meringues and the chocolate ball are delicately balanced on a kind of see-saw gizmo. The dessert is served in a 'bowl' made from half of a football, filled with remarkably aromatic artificial turf.

At prescribed moments in the recording, Gopnik is instructed to eat a meringue; then a second, more intensely flavoured than the first; and then the third, the most intense of all. When he eats this last, the see-saw's balance is destroyed and the chocolate 'football' is somehow flung high in the air and dropped into a spun-candy 'net', just as the recording shrieks 'MESSI! GOOOOOOAL!' Gopnik reports:

> You feel . . . something of what Messi must feel: first, the
> overwhelming presence of the grass beneath his feet . . .
> then the tentative elegance of acquired skill, represented

by the stepladder of the perfumed meringues; and,
finally, the infantile joy, the childlike release, of scoring,
represented by the passion-fruit cream and the candy-store
pop rocks

that fill the football that you eat after it drops into the net.[1] That
chic place – its full name El Celler de Can Roca – describes itself
as a 'free-style restaurant, committed to the avant-garde', a place
whose 'link to academia has led it to defend the dialogue between
the countryside and science, a total dialogue'.[2] What Gopnik
describes is an experience that is every bit as aesthetic as it is
gustatory. El Celler's chefs seek purposely to be creative; the restaurant's style falls under the heading of what is sometimes called
'molecular gastronomy'. This culinary movement draws upon the
findings of food science and sensory science to create unusual,
sensation-rich, frequently witty, often esoteric and pretty much
always fabulously expensive dishes.

Eight time zones away and a couple of decades earlier,
Alice Waters launched what she called 'A Delicious Revolution'.
From her base at San Francisco's Chez Panisse restaurant she was
influential in kick-starting the local foods revival in the United
States. As that movement gained steam in more recent years,
Waters took on a new goal: to extend the reach of the Delicious
Revolution to school cafeterias, making the food in them health-
ful, safe and tasty.

What could be a more delicious revolution than to start
committing our best resources to teaching this [how to
make good food choices] to children – by feeding them
and giving them pleasure; by teaching them how to grow
food responsibly; and by teaching them how to cook it and
eat it, together, around the table? . . . Food seduces you by
its very nature – the smell of baking, for example: It makes
you hungry! Who could resist the aroma of fresh bread, or
the smell of warm tortillas coming off the comal?[3]

Waters drew inspiration from farmer, novelist, essayist and food activist Wendell Berry. His essay 'The Pleasures of Eating' (1989) bemoaned the move from eating as an 'agricultural act' to eating as an 'industrial' one. He encouraged readers to cultivate what he called an 'extensive pleasure' in their food. This pleasure comes from being able to understand and smile with approval at the conditions under which the foodstuffs in a meal were grown and produced. The delight – the aesthetic appreciation – one takes in this food can best arise, says Berry, when one knows *and approves of* the conditions under which one's food was grown.[4]

Aesthetic pleasure is, therefore, the result of novelty, creativity, play and careful choreography, as at El Celler; or, it arises from knowing where the food on your plate was grown, as according to Berry and Waters. These very different positions share an important assumption that is by no means a conceptual given: eating should not be a dull, merely biological act. It is not just a means by which one passes appropriate nutrients into a particular physiological vessel. But *how* to move beyond the merely physiological? Which elements of the cycle 'from ground to gut' get to count as *aesthetically* relevant? What should be emphasized as part of the fuller experience that deserves to be described as 'aesthetic?' And – to thicken the plot – if food is aesthetically valuable, does that make it art?

A third story further complicates these questions. After a day of being escorted on errands and tourism in Accra, the frenetic capital of Ghana, Lisa and her travelling companion Ellen ask if they can treat their host to lunch, 'you pick the place.' The young, hip, college woman's choice: a newly opened KFC. The line at the restaurant was out the door with mostly young Ghanaians, anxious to get their first taste of the iconic American brand. So, on their second day in Ghana, the Americans abroad found themselves waiting in line to order a quintessentially American fast-food meal – ironically, one they wouldn't likely eat at home. When they finally sat down to plates of very familiar looking poultry and fries and cups of very familiar tasting Diet Coke, the foods' emblematic and unsubtle flavours transported them . . . home. After an enjoyable but admittedly gruelling day in an intense, exciting, vibrant but daunting city in which it was hard not to be reminded at every turn that they were white, comparatively wealthy and American, it was *also* hard not to take pleasure in the air-conditioned comfort of the entire KFC experience.

How to characterize the food part of that experience? Well, in familiar terms: salty, crispy, greasy, metallic-acidic and refrigerated. Nothing of molecular cuisine about the place. No concerns about animal welfare, locally sourced produce or healthy food choices, either. Overall, though, quite pleasurable (there's something about a French fry . . .) and, let's face it, aesthetically appealing in its own salty, metallic way.

As these three examples suggest, the contemporary food world includes a wide array of trends, movements, industries. These exist alongside each other and may jostle for our attention as eaters. At the same time, they can also tend to occupy separate spheres, appealing to almost entirely different audiences and bumping into each other rather less than one might expect. (Income, for one thing, determines to a great degree who can have which experiences.) The net effect is that these different approaches to food and agriculture offer varying conceptions of food, of taste, of pleasure.

These distinct approaches are the source of the food 'mess' that sets the context for this chapter on food, art and the aesthetic. Each approach can be associated with particular aesthetic commitments or sensibilities; with ways of thinking about the aesthetic and artistic value of food. These ways of thinking, like the approaches to food that give rise to them are, to be sure, not consistent with one another and are in fact sometimes downright contradictory. (There's no KFC at a Delicious Revolutionary elementary school.) Purists and ideologues can always straighten out contradictions by oversimplifying or decreeing. For those of a more conflicted temperament, tugged in different directions, it's a bit harder. The result: a philosophical mess.

What Makes Art Art?

To understand this mess requires sifting through the layers comprising it. We start with the word 'art' itself. In the past few centuries 'art' has been set against 'craft' and come to hold an exalted, honorific status. This is a result of the term being embedded within a philosophical context that springs from the generative idea of mind–body dualism and the associated theory/practice dichotomy discussed in Chapter One. Art, in this view, is and should – unlike craft – be of no practical use. Works of art are not 'for' anything other than aesthetic appreciation. In this definition, food has a very difficult time claiming membership of the category 'art'. Its usefulness, after all, is unavoidable.

Of the three examples with which we began, the one that most clearly represents an attempt to treat food as 'art' and to emphasize its cousin, 'creativity', comes from the haute cuisine restaurant. At El Celler, as at other exquisite – and exquisitely expensive – 'dining galleries', chefs create elaborate 'works of food', clearly informed by works of art, whose main focus is quite removed from the mundane task of nourishing people. (Indeed, nourishment could not be more beside the point, a fact that has led some diners to quip that they felt like they needed to stop on the way back to their hotel for a hamburger, because they weren't quite full after their meal.)

Diners require a sizeable amount of sophistication to fully appreciate the creativity and ingenuity represented in the dishes. Food might be the material, but art is the product; these chefs have moved their creations beyond the ('subordinate') realm of 'craft'. Having lifted their efforts beyond answering to mere biological necessity, such chefs allow diners to remove themselves from the routine, everyday world. They produce creations that are visually wonderful, perhaps as much as they are delicious. Hervé

This, a chemist who specializes in the physical chemistry of cooking, has said it directly: he admires the inventive cooks whose aim 'is not to fill up the stomach of their guests but to produce culinary art'.[5]

There is a general inclination (among 'foodies', to be sure, but among the rest of us as well) to assume that the El Celler experience closely approximates 'art'. This seems natural enough. Art, on the view we have inherited, is about something exalted, something susceptible to a special kind of experience – the aesthetic. This kind of experience must, in an important way, remove us from the everyday, prosaic reality of (bodily) human life. If food is to be art it must minimize or disguise its utilitarian associations with feeding that body. Otherwise, it might just as well give up aspiring to the realm of the aesthetic. Art, the definition tells us, must be set aside from whatever is practical.

Philosophers specialize in asking questions about topics that everyone else assumes to be settled – a tendency that leads to receiving fewer dinner party invitations than we might like. (Who wants their dinner party conversation shaped by someone who is the equivalent of a highly verbal two year old, continually asking 'why?') The apparently settled question we ask here: 'what is art?'

Our reason for asking questions whose answers seem obvious has to do with the nature of philosophy as we understand it. Basing itself in intellectual history, philosophy begins with a guiding assumption: any important term has gathered around itself a set of connotations associated with a particular time and place. Those connotations together give rise to the focal meanings that the term has at present. In this particular case, 'art' carries associations with concepts such as beauty, refinement, permanence, appreciation, detachment, museum. This dominant cluster of connotations obviously favours, or at least suggests, the centrality of certain arts over others. Ask people who their favourite artists are, for instance, and very often they will reply with names such as Monet, Cézanne, Goya, Rembrandt: in other words, *painters*. Why, philosophers ask, has painting moved to the centre of what we mean by 'art'? The ancient Greeks or the medievals would not have identified art with painting. Literature, architecture and music would have been more likely candidates.

Terms like 'art' and 'aesthetic' are embedded within a kind of semantic landscape. Philosophers, tracking the shifting landscapes in the history of ideas, come to a double realization: first, key terms have not always had the same meanings as they do now; second, it is always important to examine the entrenched meanings associated with key terms. This second move will allow us to determine whether a now-sedimented meaning has come to be constricting; whether it has come to limit, unnecessarily, the possibilities for answering the question 'what is art?'

The philosophical practice of revisiting entrenched meanings has a companion practice within the sciences, where concepts also accumulate connotations that can come to be limiting. The word 'atom', for instance, once had a perfectly clear meaning: that which is indivisible. (This is exactly what the etymology means: *a*, not, *tomos*, cut). Several centuries and several paradigm shifts later, the word 'atom' remains but, because of its new semantic landscape, it no longer has the same connotations, or even the same denotations as it once did. Whereas Democritus (460–370 BCE) made a metaphysical stipulation of great import when he defined the atom as the smallest particle that can exist, in the contemporary world we can barely open the day's newspaper without reading that another *sub*atomic particle has been discovered. There could have been no 'sub' for Democritus. The 'a-tom' is indivisible; Q.E.D.

This example, which represents such a clear case of altered and expanded meaning, can help us notice the less sharp ways in which such a process has affected the term 'art'. The predominant meaning of this term has been inherited from a time in which the stomach, its functions and its associated activities were all relegated to the intellectual margins, outside the realm of polite philosophical conversation. Undergirding this now solidly sedimented way of thinking is the generative idea of mind–body dualism. This orientation gave rise, in turn, to the notion of humans as 'minds' set over and against an 'external' world. This latter becomes an 'object' which humans as minds observe, objectively and disinterestedly. John Dewey, a major influence for us, referred to this view as the 'spectator theory of knowledge'. As Dewey saw it, we think of ourselves primarily as spectators of a world of which we are literally not a part. Such a 'spectator' attitude can make perfect sense – provided we assume that the best and only way to describe the complicated human being is via the positing of two entities, mind and body. Then, 'mind' can itself be the primary spectator, looking out on its primary object, the body. Such minds, being immaterial, could not, in principle, be parts of the natural world. Their more primordial status is that of being spectators.

The spectator understanding of humans' relation to the natural world, in turn, brings with it certain ramifications for the way we conceptualize art. As noted above, a set of defining concepts emerges, including beauty, refinement, permanence, appreciation, detachment, museum. We'll take a brief look at these terms here, because eventually we will offer alternative concepts that spring more organically from the alternative generative idea that motivates us.

The modern institution of the museum arose, in part, alongside the idea that objects of art should be set aside for a particular kind of contemplation. One corollary: such objects ought to be situated in special places designed to *foster* that contemplation. ('Concert hall' would be a similar term.) The concept of detachment illustrates the belief that minds contemplating artworks must remain disconnected from those works, because such detachment enables 'objectivity', while the concept of appreciation manifests the view that works of art are the objects of a special kind of attention, to which we give the honorific name 'aesthetic appreciation'. Beauty, while 'useless' in the sense discussed at the beginning of this chapter, is also the highest aesthetic value – indeed, its value is connected to its uselessness – beauty doesn't *need* to do anything else. Refinement presumes that art is the sort of thing that appeals to the higher faculties of human beings, the rational faculties that we possess by virtue of our being 'minds'. And finally, permanence is an acknowledgement that beautiful works should persist through time; that which is fleeting is a poor candidate for the category 'art'. This means both that a work should appeal to future generations (and faraway cultures) and that the literal work is fabricated out of something that can survive.

All of this makes sense – within a particular orientation. That orientation gives rise to a consistent package in which 'art' takes on the associations mentioned above. That consistent package, in turn, comes to be restrictive and limiting when we consider what it cannot readily accommodate. Many products of non-Western artistry have to be artificially disengaged from their functional or ritualistic settings in order to be displayed in museums. The same is true for many quintessential items of Western art: Greek vases, medieval religious ritual objects, furniture and the whole array of artefacts now confined to the realm of 'craft'.

From Spectator to Farmer

When anomalous instances like these pile up, it is time to take a look at the general context within which the terms 'art' and 'aesthetic' have accumulated their contemporary meanings. It is time, in other words, to examine the philosophical plumbing. Time, really, to see what happens when we make alterations to this plumbing. Our changes do not really invent anything new. They offer new ways of reclaiming and repurposing ideas that have been part of Western thought since the ancients. Our alternate generative notion is admittedly straightforward and basic – at least straightforward and basic were it not for the historical detour of the mind *versus* body approach. Our galvanizing idea starts with flesh-and-blood humans and adds, as its unique contribution, the reminder that we are stomach-endowed. Creatures in touch with their hunger are little inclined to define themselves as outside the world – as detached, indifferent spectators contemplating its beauty at arm's length. Returning the stomach to human self-understanding might seem to be a simple move. Perhaps it is. But the complications that result from this move are anything but simple. Indeed, our motto could be 'Complexify'. The stomach, to get to the heart of the matter (mixed metaphor intended), has little patience with a notion of humans as mere spectators. The stomach is an agent of interaction and mingling. Indeed, its actual work of digestion is an instance of such interaction. Not only does it involve ingesting products from our surroundings, but the process of digestion is carried out with the assistance of helpful, resident bacteria. Hunger, and the need to satisfy it, encourage thoughtful planning, careful husbandry and concern for consequences. Creatures such as these cannot, in general, think of themselves as spectators. Nor can they remain content with a conception of art and the aesthetic that keeps beauty always at arm's length, in a museum.

As noted in Chapter One, our new generative model calls for us to replace the models of human being that came to predominate in modern philosophies. Detached spectators and geometers working with ideal triangles do not align with our recognition of the fundamental interconnectedness of humans. The farmer, the figure who connects soil and soup, is our chosen alternative. But surely we have some explaining to do, if we are to put farmers into the same sentence as the word 'art'. In a philosophical world in which art (abstract, theoretical, conceptual, mental) is sharply separated from craft (concrete, material, physical), the work of the farmer is regarded as craft work, if it is regarded as creative at all. (A big 'if' indeed; in recent Western thought, the farmer has come to stand as the emblem of simple-mindedness and lack of creativity. The recent surge of popular interest in farming and farmers has by no means yet erased this sentiment.) If we are going to link farmers and art in a meaningful way, we've got our work cut out for us.

So what *does* all this talk of humans as spectators or farmers have to do with art, with El Celler, KFC and a 'delicious revolution'? Quite a bit, as it turns out. The question 'What is art?' and its companion 'Is food art?' warrant one kind of answer when asked from within the context of a mind-centred, spectator-guided philosophy. They will be answered in quite a different way when asked from within a farmer-guided, stomach-endowed philosophy. The different way – this is important to note – is not just a matter of ethereal academic concern. It actually brings with it important ramifications for everyday life.

Hegel, Kant and Received Ideas

So, how to make the transition to a stomach-endowed way? Let us begin by returning to our three initial examples. Each provides satisfying experiences. Within our inherited philosophical conception of art, with its central notions of 'aesthetic experience' and 'art appreciation', El Celler occupies a central place. Dining at El Celler is a special experience in which one is drawn to note and appreciate the creativity and beauty of the food and surroundings. These qualities, the diner understands, are to be appreciated for their own sakes. The other two eating experiences might be comforting (KFC) or ethically admirable (Delicious Revolution), but on the received view, they do not count as 'aesthetic' experiences. Eating local is not like looking at a Rembrandt.

As we have sought to explain, such a perspective on food versus art has a distinguished intellectual history. An influential philosophical tradition has worked to fashion a context within which compartmentalization – which separates the aesthetic from the ethical from the emotional – becomes second nature. It was not always thus. A tradition that runs back to the ancients understood the aesthetic and the ethical as integrally intertwined. There is even a term, 'axiology', which refers to 'the study of value' and incorporates both ethics and aesthetics. Tearing the two apart required a particular set of intellectual moves. The sequestering of 'art' from ordinary life was a natural move within the intellectual landscape that bifurcated humans into higher and lower compartments.

To provide some elaboration, we introduce Georg Wilhelm Friedrich Hegel (1770–1831), arguably the most important Western philosopher of the nineteenth century. He laid down a basic position upon which this notion of a special arena labelled 'aesthetic' has been built. 'High' and 'low' factor importantly in his description. The 'higher' realm is, of course, the mental, associated with the head and, more particularly, the mind. 'Lower' is a kind of all-inclusive category, encompassing everything else – all those human parts that are irremediably associated with the body. Most relevant for our purposes is the fact that the higher dimension is associated with seeing and hearing. These are the senses regarded as closest to the mind-as-spectator. Their affinity is cemented by the fact that they are most comfortable with distance and detachment.

Proximity is not necessary for their proper functioning. Indeed, too close proximity is a hindrance. Operating at a distance works best for them. The other, lower senses, situating us in the gooey, sticky (let's face it), dirty, tactile realm, come to be understood (no surprise here) as distractions that draw us away from the upward trajectory that is our human birthright. As the theorist Laura Marks observes, 'Hegel argued that aesthetics is the transcendent rise from a sensuous particular to a universal truth, and was only possible through the distance senses: "smell, taste and touch have to do with matter as such and its immediately sensuous qualities . . .".'[6] Hegel, being fully consistent, states the position directly: 'For this reason these [proximate] senses cannot have to do with artistic objects, which are meant to maintain themselves in their real independence and allow of no *purely* sensuous relationship. What is agreeable for these senses is not the beauty of art.'[7]

It is hard to be more straightforward. Hegel did not explicitly use the words, but he might as well have said: 'food can never aspire to the status of art.' Food is sunken in the world of touch, smell and taste. There is no way it can arrive at universality or transcendence. We can marvel all we want at the wonders produced by someone like Takayo Kiyota, a 'sushi artist', whose creations, images that emerge when the sushi roll is sliced open, may be 'just too beautiful to eat',[8] but in the end they can be eaten. Even if vision is an important element in sushi art, this is not good enough. At least, not good enough from the Hegelian perspective. As long as her works are edible, they remain in the realm of what are called the 'proximate' senses (as contrasted to the distal – a distinction we will discuss more in the next chapter). This realm – of touch, taste and smell – is immersed in the domain of the here and now, a sunkenness that negates the very possibilities for 'the transcendent rise from a sensuous particular to a universal truth', as Marks put it.

Even the folks at El Celler would get a 'nice try, but you just don't get it, do you?' The talented chefs at that restaurant can be quite playful and innovative. They use food in ways that we could even describe as moving us closer to the level of the universal; their dishes are deeply conceptual, intellectual, they draw attention not only to the visual but to the auditory. They even get marks for not aiming to 'fill you up', and they are not at all concerned with anything as prosaic as nutrition. They use food in ways that move us closer to the level of the transcendent. Nevertheless, to an adherent of the received philosophy of art, such a move is compromised as long as it remains even tangentially associated with actual eating.

By definition, creations designed to be appreciated with one's mouth cannot belong to the realm of 'higher' objects intended for disinterested aesthetic appreciation. Never mind that the mouth and nose, like the eyes and ears, are located in the head, a location that *should* earn them some status. No matter; the mouth must come in contact with its object in order to taste it. And the nose? Well, that's a good question. Noses, like eyes, *seem* to operate at a distance, but (perhaps) because of the nose's close association with the mouth, it too is treated as a proximate sense. So, too, is touch, another sense that is often involved in a complete experience of eating. But it is the involvement of the mouth most of all that seems to doom food, to trap it, to guarantee that it cannot be anything more than a prosaic craft, at best. The mouth, of course, is a direct path to the stomach.

In emphasizing the higher realms to which genuine art reaches, Hegel underscored some famous remarks on art made by Kant. For Kant, 'the aesthetic' was actually a realm unto itself, one whose main concern was beauty. But, being a philosopher of a particular, stomach-blocking kind, what Kant meant by beauty and the recognition of beauty was far from ordinary experience. In that, we are involved as concerned participants. Decidedly more spectator than farmer, Kant, first of all, demands that a real aesthetic judgement be 'disinterested', meaning detached, dispassionate, disengaged. Right away we know the stomach is not involved. Farmers, whose efforts are directly and indirectly connected to the needs of the stomach, are, by the nature of their occupation, interested and engaged, not neutral or dispassionate.

Second, for Kant, there is a *kind* of universality to aesthetic judgements. If someone makes the claim that X is beautiful, then this should be a universally valid claim, true for all 'rational agents' (Kant's rather tortured term for 'humans and anyone else who can think like one'). The claim of beauty must be true everywhere and at all times. Once again, the stomach moves us in a different direction. Humans, over time and place, have exhibited many different tastes, created multiple cuisines, manifested all sorts of predilections and aversions for food. Universal agreements on matters of taste, beyond very basic ones, such as the human predisposition for sweetness, tend to be rare. More common, where the stomach is concerned, is a multiplicity of tastes.

As if he purposely wanted to position himself as a foil for us, Kant specifically excludes from the aesthetic realm any pleasurable feelings derived from food and drink. Moreover, to guarantee beyond a shadow of a doubt that food cannot slip its way into the category of the aesthetic, he excludes from it any judgements having to do with the good. As Kant sees it, when the (ethically) good is involved, disinterestedness goes out the window.[9] The deliciousness extolled by the so-called 'Delicious Revolution' could never be accepted into the aesthetic category. This is because it is so clearly a moral category, concerned with making food 'good' in a whole host of senses, including nutritionally, environmentally and socio-politically, in addition to 'mouthily'.

Kant is centuries removed from us, but his influence lingers. Think of a museum visit, perhaps the quintessential instance of aesthetic appreciation, at least within highbrow layers of Western society. Such an experience reveals how much our ways of thinking about art have been shaped by Kantian approaches to it. We enter a museum and by doing so leave ordinary life, its cares and worries, its *interests*, behind. As we admire the paintings, sculptures and other 'aesthetic' objects, we contemplate them in terms of their beauty. We focus on the matter of their (abstract) beauty even when the objects displayed are vases, snuff boxes or clothing, quite utilitarian objects when seen in context. 'Proper' museumgoers know that we must bracket their utility, so that we can concentrate on their 'truly aesthetic' virtues. The function they used to serve, the purpose for which they once were 'good', is of no aesthetic interest to the museum spectator. Indeed, considerations of function can get in the way. Only as long as their utilitarian dimensions are ignored (or recognized, perhaps, but only as curiosities), are they worthy of display and appreciation. In other words, as long as they can be made to approximate the arts best suited to spectators – sculpture and, especially, painting – then clothing and snuff boxes can be accommodated in the realm of the aesthetic.

This kind of bracketing has been especially apparent – and especially egregious – when beautiful-and-utilitarian objects from non-Western cultures have been placed in Western art museums. From a Kantian vantage point, the 'elevating' of such works via museum displays is unquestionably a way of honouring them

– an acknowledgement that these objects manifest the universal qualities of beauty to which Kant's view is committed. From our vantage point, the egregiousness stems in part from the fact that turning the objects into 'art' requires ripping them from contexts in which they 'make sense' and have meaning. This has to be done in order to insert them into a setting in which that very meaning *must* be set aside so that their 'purely aesthetic' (and purportedly universal) qualities can be appreciated.

The Hegelian/Kantian take on art separates what it regards as genuine art from spurious wannabes. It also gives grounds upon which to allow admission of other 'art-like' creations – for example, beautiful but useful objects created in cultures with no separate category of (intentionally non-utilitarian) works of art, or objects that somehow manage to 'transcend' their usefulness to become artworks in spite of themselves. What makes art *art*? *Genuine* art is marked by various levels of sequestering. The body of the art viewer must be isolated – in a museum or concert hall, say – to make room for elevation to the universal and spiritual (Hegel). Concerns of everyday life must be left behind as preparation for a properly 'aesthetic' experience (Kant).

Such moves are just the sort we would expect to arise from the spectator approach. Indeed, the discipline of philosophy is useful here in helping us notice how clusters of concepts go together because they occupy some shared intellectual landscape. In order for the views on art enunciated by Kant and Hegel even to be considered as options, let alone come to predominate, a prior shift had to occur in defining the contours of the setting within which the human condition was understood. Within that setting, flesh-and-blood, stomach-endowed human beings faded to the background. They were replaced by spectators, beings that René Descartes (1596–1650) called 'thinking things'. All of a sudden the main human activity was not, well, activity, but *cogitation*.

Given the rise of this paradigm, it is not surprising that, when asked to name 'artists', many of us in the West reply with a list of painters. Painting is an art highly congenial to the spectator stance. It can readily be accommodated in the disinterested realm of museums. It can be understood as helping transport us beyond the immediate senses to the key distal one, vision (you never lick or touch a painting, or even smell it, at least not in order to appreciate it aesthetically). Painting can even aspire to be a purely 'spiritual' medium, as the paintings and writings of Wassily Kandinsky demonstrated.[10]

Recall that we set out to show how we could develop a new generative idea that places our stomach-endowed nature at its heart, one that replaces the geometer-spectator with the farmer as a model for human being. We excavated the older generative idea, with its emphasis on a division between 'higher' (vision) and 'lower' (taste) senses, higher (art) and lower (craft) forms of human activity. And we examined the conception of art that rests upon this generative idea, a conception that emphasizes disembodied, dispassionate appreciation at a distance, the paradigm that fixes on painting and other visual arts as its quintessential examples. The older generative idea has no room whatsoever for food as art. We can see quite clearly now the resources we must gather in order to consolidate an alternative generative idea, one that will support a robust conception of food as aesthetically significant – perhaps even of food as art. We now turn to the next stage of that task, considering the work of a contemporary thinker who can be called one of the first true aestheticians of food – that is, someone who intentionally set out to investigate and discuss food philosophically.

Contemporary Philosophy, Art, Food: Carolyn Korsmeyer

In the latter decades of the twentieth century, aesthetic theory was challenged by an individual who dared to bring food and philosophy into conversation: Carolyn Korsmeyer.[11] Her *Making Sense of Taste* (1999) strikes a strong, if indirect, blow against the dominant model of aesthetics, the generative mind–body dualism on which it rests, and the hierarchy of the senses to which that dualism gives rise. Korsmeyer does much to challenge the familiar dismissal of the proximate senses, and especially to rehabilitate taste. Indeed, as the title of her book suggests, this rehabilitation or reclamation process is a major emphasis. She also considers, more peripherally, the question 'is food art – or *could* it be art?' She argues that a meal can indeed meet some of the central criteria of an artwork: 'reference, representation, expression, exemplification and the social conditions of its preparation and serving'.[12] These criteria are most emphatically and robustly met in important ritual meals such as Thanksgiving in the u.s. or the Jewish Seder.

When it comes to answering the question of whether food *is* an art form, however, Korsmeyer is cautious. She, like we, notes the Western tradition's insistence on divisions between art and craft, between the fine and the applied arts – divisions that spring quite directly from the mind–body dualism. In the end, though, she argues that the exaggerated bifurcation can be corrected without falling into what she regards as the trap of overstatement by declaring food a fine art. As she puts it, 'I do not want to try to level the senses or their objects in such a way that the traditions that rank the senses disappear altogether.'[13] Given the heritage of Western philosophy, and following the hierarchy that places distal above proximate senses, 'food does not qualify as a fine art.'[14] Korsmeyer is willing to preserve that notion of fine art, while also acknowledging that 'culinary art can still be considered a minor or decorative art, or perhaps a functional or applied art.'[15] She does not reject the claim that food is art because of something intrinsic or inherent about food or tasting or smelling. Rather, she rejects the categorization because of something about history, about the way that both food and art have emerged as cultural practices.

Here she is on to something important. Korsmeyer argues that 'art' is just too narrow a category to encompass all that food is and can be, aesthetically. We'd be doing food a disservice to reduce its many qualities so that it would fit into the category of 'art'. In effecting this move, Korsmeyer indicates that the problem may not be so much with food as with the philosophical inheritance that gave us a particular understanding of 'art'. Maybe the category of 'fine art' isn't so fine after all.

In declining to grant 'art' status to food, Korsmeyer is not simply inheriting the fallout from the old, problematic generative idea; she is suggesting that, given the restrictiveness of the category, granting art status to food is not the most efficacious thing we can do to recognize and value it aesthetically. Far more important is the task of rescuing food from the dustbin of general aesthetic insignificance to which it was relegated because of its close association with the body and with what were considered the least intellectual of the senses. Undertaking this rescue work enables us to begin to understand the far greater aesthetic potential that food can have – potential that extends beyond the category of 'art'. Admitting and appreciating food's particular place within the sphere of the aesthetic is the more important aspect. Both art and food form complex 'symbolic systems'[16] that can carry important aesthetic meaning and value to those who experience them.

Korsmeyer shows that foods and eating experiences routinely manifest symbolic meaning that can be aesthetically rich. Chicken soup, to choose an intentionally prosaic example, *expresses* (a particular kind of symbolic move) comfort, both figuratively and literally. The figurative comforts it expresses are connected, integrally, to its physical ones; the reason chicken soup is a metaphorical balm for the soul is that it is a physiological balm for congested nasal passages and bronchia. While not the most aesthetically fascinating example, the case of chicken soup illustrates the ways in which ordinary foods of all sorts – pretzels, candy corn, apples, dumplings, salted meat – can have meanings that carry aesthetic weight (sometimes important aesthetic weight).

Reading Korsmeyer's argument about the deeply cultural nature of categories such as art, one is led to reflect on the ways in which cultural institutions like art museums often do violence to the works of another culture, by, for example, defining the latter's ceremonial, ritual or everyday objects as 'fine art' in an attempt to show respect to them. The intention may have been to honour them, but in applying the category of 'fine art', which did not exist in the other culture, the real result is distortion. (In eras that are, we hope, now coming to a close, those with the power to anoint something as a work of art – curators, critics, artists – often disregarded the fact that such 'respect' often felt like deep disrespect, even violence, to members of the cultures from which these objects were extracted.) Ceremonial, ritual, even well-fashioned everyday objects can be understood as aesthetic in a wider sense that we support, but this is different from their being displayed in a museum as objects of a special kind of contemplation. When it comes to food, we would impoverish it, not elevate it, were we required to understand it only in the terms afforded us by the category of fine art.

A Different Conception of Art

While we appreciate Korsmeyer's aesthetic rescue of food, we believe that something more could happen if we were to correct traditional philosophy's artificial bracketing of the stomach. Once we destabilize the entire 'spectator'-centred approach, the possibility arises for rethinking the meanings of both 'art' and even 'philosophy' itself. One important result: a different way of thinking about food as art. For Korsmeyer, once we assume the traditional and historically situated assumptions, then food preparation must automatically fall into the category of a lesser art. We believe that, when one starts one's aesthetic thinking *from* food (rather than thinking *about* food using received aesthetic categories), one cannot but reconsider some deeply imbedded assumptions about the definition of 'art' itself.

What exactly are we suggesting? Let's be clear about one thing. We agree with Korsmeyer that inverting things and moving the arts of cookery to the highest rank is the wrong strategy. Our shift to a different generative idea is a different kind of move. First, emphasizing our stomach-endowedness forces us to understand ourselves as involved in engaged, interested, concerned interactions *in* the world. Second, it also makes central the role of taste (tasting, that is – not the aesthetic sense). We are bodily, savouring creatures (*Homo sapiens*). We experience certain foods pleasurably, others somewhat neutrally, still others with displeasure, even disgust. These two features, involvement and taste, warrant a quite different approach to the whole relationship between art and food.

Aesthetic Experiences are Consummatory Experiences

Given our revised generative idea, the focus is no longer on preserving a distinction between art and craft. Rather, it centres on a notion we borrow from John Dewey, that of 'consummatory experiences'.[17] Such experiences are not simple, immediate sensations of pleasure or displeasure ('chocolate!' or 'gritty!'). Nor are they monitored by a simple on/off switch ('art', 'not art'). Rather, they are characterized by layers of ingredients and energies that build to a kind of culmination that, itself, admits of degrees. Consummatory experiences are on a continuum rather than bifurcated. They can be characterized as having a certain 'rightness' that emerges from the mix of ingredients along with a sense of satisfying achievement, rather than an abrupt termination. Instead of demanding, as a precondition for the aesthetic, an emphasis on isolated purity (the museum, the concert hall), the model we propose emphasizes inclusiveness. In addition, as its name suggests, it emphasizes experiencing, a *process* of connection or interaction, not a static state or an independent object. While the Hegel/Kant-inspired notion of art was associated with the concepts of beauty, refinement, permanence, appreciation, detachment, museum, our alternative model will emphasize, as ingredients of the consummatory, the notions of combination, situation, attraction, temporality and fineness.

The Hegel/Kant approach had been built upon a basic negativity. Its pivotal concept was the *not*: *not* in everyday experience, *not* related to the proximate senses, *not* useful, *not* ethical. Our alternative will emphasize *and*: delightful, *and* useful, *and* beautiful, *and* good. The highest degrees of aesthetic experience will maximize the possibilities of the *and* dimension. A well-written, well-performed play can pull this off. So can a well-designed building, a poem and a painting. So, too, can a good meal. Any creative endeavour might achieve these levels. Any of these creative forms can also *fail* to achieve the highest levels of excellence; no single kind of endeavour is guaranteed to achieve those levels. The rigid boundary separating art from not art has just been rendered a permeable membrane.

Given the new prototype (a focus on experience rather than object; insistence on the *and*), some new concepts emerge as definitive. 'Combination', which represents the 'and' dimension, is one. Another is 'situation'. Whereas the notion of art to which we are responding emphasized the importance of creating special places in which to engage in 'aesthetic appreciation', our notion emphasizes the fact that a consummatory experience is the result of a confluence of factors that compose actual lived circumstances. Rather than requiring certain kinds of created objects, or certain kinds of rarefied settings, our view begins from the understanding that one could have a consummatory experience rooted in a mundane object – a bowl of chicken soup, for example – if the context creates the right sort of situation. It is 'attractive' in that it literally draws us into it, allows an experience in which we are not constantly checking our phone for the latest texts or status updates. The experience itself is not that of an isolated instant, but is spread out over a span of time. 'Temporality', understood as both a stretch of time and as indicating the importance of the particular era or epoch in which the experience is unfolding, replaces the atemporal universality prominent in the

Hegel/Kant understanding of art. Likewise, a situation could fail to materialize even in the presence of an object that has inspired millions – a crowded, touristy jostle through the Sistine Chapel, for example.

'Consummatory experiences happen' might be our motto. Certain kinds of objects are obviously designed in order to make them happen, and certain kinds of contexts are devised to enable them – but those are just special cases of a more general case, rather than the defining conditions for art and for experiences characterized as aesthetic. Sometimes a bowl of chicken soup will be consummatory; sometimes it's just lunch.

Another new concept to which this notion of art gives rise speaks to the older separation of the fine from the applied arts. Within our prototype, modes of discrimination and distinction are preserved. What changes is the automatic identification of superiority or fineness with a particular kind of activity, and the automatic relegation to inferiority of others such as furniture making, pottery or weaving. Fineness (a clumsy word of the sort to which philosophy is sometimes forced to resort) becomes a matter of artistry aiming at the fullest sorts of combinations. Not only are these combinations of materials used in fabrication but, in addition, they are modes of combining the beautiful, the useful and the good. Artistry is about weaving together possibilities that once seemed incompatible. It is not about disinterest, pure beauty or leaving the material realm for the spiritual. (For that matter, it is not about leaving the spiritual realm for the material; the notion that these two 'substances' can be understood as distinct is part of the very problem.)

In this way, some standard associations are retained, albeit in reformulated ways. The inherent enjoyment that is part and parcel of an aesthetic experience has not been set aside. One aspect of consummatory experiences is that they are pleasurable. But recalling the *and* dimension helps remind us that there are fine enjoyments, as there are crude pleasures. The elegance and success of the mixtures and conjunctions will determine the degree of consummation occasioned by the experience. What is aesthetic will be pleasurable (in some sense of that word), although what is pleasurable may not be aesthetic.[18] Once again the conjointness, the 'and' dimension, becomes a key marker.

Within the approach that holds that we are really just minds attached to bodies, the *not* factor predominates. Within such a perspective, pleasures integrating a bodily component fall under the dismissive heading of 'hedonic'. Such pleasures automatically include the stomach- and mouth-centred pleasure of a meal. Note: automatically. This, we think, is a mistake. It is not the making of distinctions that carries the flaw, but the way those distinctions are carved out. A better approach, one that insists on artistry and fineness, along with the *and* factor, carves out distinctions differently. It recognizes many arts – that is, many modes of fabrication. Each of them conjoins possibilities in new and harmonious ways.

Fineness is not inevitably associated with some arts and dismissive of others (even though some arts might have a longer and deeper history of practicing the search for fineness). How comprehensive are the various possibilities that seek to be woven together? How well does a work manage to combine the varied components? Is there concordance in the composition? Are beauty, meaning, goodness and utility present in the blend? If so, there is fineness. Even better, there is fullness of an aesthetic experience *to the degree* in which beauty, meaning, goodness and utility are woven together.

Participation and the Consummatory

When such a scheme is applied to cuisine, some surprising results occur. A meal of comfort food that gets the simple elements of ingredients, setting and company just right can be a consummatory, and thus aesthetic, experience: think candlelight, creamy potato soup, homemade bread and a circle of friends on a cold winter night. On the other hand, the world of haute cuisine need not automatically emerge as prototypically aesthetically important (even though it is the world that most self-consciously seeks to create works that would be defined as art according to the spectator theory). If the particular 'eating event' is composed of elaborate fabrications that are, for instance, constructed with disdain for the matter of nourishing people, if they are best 'savoured' by contemplating or standing back in detached appreciation, then they are peripheral, rather than central to the circle of aesthetic experiences. Such works – the creations of the pastry chef at El Celler, for instance, or the inventions of chefs at El Bulli or the Fat Duck or French Laundry, or any other exquisite, exquisitely expensive 'dining gallery' – would be closer to 'art' on the Hegel/ Kant scale. On our scale, though, they remain within the meaning horizon in which value depends on separating fine from applied art, daily life from refined detachment, the nutritious from the spiritual.

The emphasis on integrated experience reiterates our point that the aesthetic now connotes the entire situation. The isolated individual confronting an object in a rarefied atmosphere (the 'museum' conception of art) becomes the exception, not the rule. Instructive here are the words of Jean Anthelme Brillat-Savarin (1755–1826), a lawyer who gained fame as a writer on gastronomy. He wrote not of the 'pleasures of eating' but of the 'pleasures of the table', which include good companionship and comfortable surroundings.[19] The aesthetics of dinner are not just confined to the sequence of dishes.

Moving beyond the dinner table, consider the legendary recording of Duke Ellington's 'Diminuendo and Crescendo in Blue' (1937) as it appears on the live album *Ellington at Newport* (1956). The recording includes sounds from the crowd and the band members, each group responding to the other and to the music as it unfolds. Listening to it, we get a sense of being in the audience watching the band members play. The fuller experience would have involved actually being there, listening to the musicians moving, shouting and cheering with the rest of the crowd, noticing how the musicians' bodies moved while they played. Other senses too, would enter into our experience, including the proximate ones. Smells were no doubt significant: cigarette smoke, marijuana, beer, sweat, aftershave, perfume. Touch as well; the size of the crowd would have meant that accidental jostling was inevitable, and the intoxicating nature of the music might likely have led to some more intentional bumping and rubbing.

Detached, spiritual 'aesthetic appreciators' would rule out much that is consummatory in this experience. To disregard the setting and the conjunction of sensations as irrelevant to the aesthetic appreciation of this music would be a major error. The 'extraneous' shouts; the white tuxedo and squinted-shut eyes of saxophonist Paul Gonsalves playing that epic 27-chorus solo; the woman from the front row of the audience who jumped on stage, gyrating – all of these *were* that performance of 'Diminuendo in Blue' and 'Crescendo in Blue'. The error of disregarding them arises from the philosophical outlook that assumes separation is better than conjunction.

We can of course listen to the recording at home or in the car. We could probably even get a recording that removes the crowd noise. What we then get is certainly a decent musical experience, but a lessened one; a distant, weakened sense of the consummatory aesthetic experience whose fullness required the crowd, the noise, the smells, the tactility. For the Hegel/Kant approach, the recording in the car, allowing a bracketed, less bodily experience, would be the more 'aesthetic' one. Or perhaps it is this: for the Hegel/Kant approach, the highest aesthetic experiences are just those that are *improved* by such bracketing. The sweaty, emotional mayhem of a live jazz concert could never attain such heights, and a sanitized recording only proves that fact. Our approach reverses this trajectory.

The Many and the Fine

In general, our table-centred model not only complexifies where others simplify, but it pluralizes where others monopolize. A great dish always comes in multiple versions. No single cuisine is *the* cuisine of the world. Indeed there is no such thing as 'cuisine', only many cuisines. In a similar manner it is a limiting error, one that distorts the complexity of human fabrications, to speak of Art with an upper case 'A'. Ballet, landscape gardening, jazz, architecture, cooking, pottery, couture, sculpture: all form part of a heterogeneous family.

Such a pluralizing, as we keep insisting, need not be accompanied by an abandonment of evaluative merits. Distinctions, including the use of 'higher' and 'lower', do not disappear. They are rethought in important ways. The big difference is that these terms are no longer tied to particular *kinds* of art. It will not necessarily be the case, for example, that painting is a higher art than architecture. Various arts serve different functions. Blanket hierarchizations rooted in kinds of art can no longer be justified.

Instead of blanket hierarchizations, our scale of distinction involves degrees of fineness. Fineness in artistic achievement involves bringing together as *compossibles* what had previously been considered *impossibles*. Consider this artistic context: an iconic Paris bridge (the Pont Neuf), yards of silky, sandstone-coloured fabric, and the demand that traffic not be interrupted in the creation of an artwork. This seemingly impossible set of circumstances is just the sort of artistic setting that inspires the artists Christo and Jeanne-Claude; their *The Pont Neuf Wrapped* (1985) and their numerous other large-scale installations provide vivid illustrations of what we might call 'compossibility'. (The fact that Christo and Jeanne-Claude's works have often been controversial – the fact that disputes have raged over whether or not they are truly 'art' – comes with the territory when you bring together impossibles. Fineness is not incompatible with controversy.)

Artists show us that combinations we believed impossible, or which we would never have conceived, can be brought about. Artistry in the traditional sense of that term stands as a ready model, an aspirational dimension in human life. This bringing together of elements, continuous with the circumstances in which works are situated, constitutes the conditions for the consummatory experience we are calling aesthetic.

The older art/craft segregation made it almost impossible for cooking to be anything other than a craft. When it was moved to the realm of fine art, it could only occupy the position of a minor art. It is true that some artists do wonderful things with materials typically associated with the table. Viviane Le Courtois utilizes foodstuffs in lovely and creative ways. A museum description of her work gives some indication of this range:

> The earliest works in the exhibition, executed in France in the 1990s before her move to the u.s., include an installation of chewed licorice sticks as well as photographs and video documentation of performances and sculptural work made from foraged foods, fruit peelings, and nut shells. For a series of *Pickles* from the early 2000s, Le Courtois filled over 200 jars with various liquids and random objects in memory of her then recently-deceased mother, who had a tendency to keep pickle jars long after the contents had been consumed.[20]

In such cases, foods are used as the material for making aesthetic works. Their 'foodiness' is, to an extent, bracketed. Appreciating the art involves doing something very different from eating it. One spectates. The works are regarded as appropriate for the museum or the performance hall. As such, these kinds of works serve as exceptions to the rule. Even a sharp critic of food as art would relent enough to allow them into the general category of art. William Deresiewicz, for instance, provides clear, direct and impassioned arguments for separating food and art. It is true, he admits, that both food and art address the senses. This, though, is

> where food stops. It is not narrative or representational, does not organize and express emotion. An apple is not

a story, even if we can tell a story about it. A curry is not an idea, even if its creation is the result of one. Meals can evoke emotions, but only very roughly and generally, and only within a very limited range – comfort, delight, perhaps nostalgia, but not anger, say, or sorrow, or a thousand other things. Food is highly developed as a system of sensations, extremely crude as a system of symbols. Proust on the madeleine is art; the madeleine itself is not art.[21]

While, as we have just mentioned, such criteria do not automatically rule out artists like Le Courtois, they do automatically rule out the examples given at the beginning of this chapter. As the scholar Aaron Meskin has pointed out, the use of foods as materials with which to make genuine art has typically been given a pass.[22] Within the Hegel/Kant model, food and art can intersect, but only when foodstuffs are used as materials for art.

Our scale of values does not dismiss so readily. It suggests that we judge on the basis of fineness *within* the various arts. We have no trouble joining the writer Mark Winegardner in his criticism of the food on which he was raised. Cooking in his childhood home involved 'slapping a half-thawed pound of hamburger in a skillet and then, while the meat fried, figuring out whether to add Campbell's Cream of Mushroom soup, Kraft mac 'n' cheese, or canned tuna.'[23] Delightful, *and* delicious, *and* nutritious, *and* inviting, *and* creative, *and* achieving a special level of attainment, such a meal as this is likely not.

Winegardner's meals offer an easy target. Pointing out their failure to be 'fine' is to shoot the proverbial fish in a barrel. What about some harder cases? What about the meals mentioned at the beginning of this chapter? How would we, living out the consequences of our new generative idea, consider them? The answers might be surprising. Let's recapitulate our position: there are many arts; the art/craft distinction has been muddled; what separates clumsy from distinguished arts is a degree of fineness; fineness is characterized by a combination of artistry and experience; fineness in artistry depends on how well an artist manages to incorporate dimensions once thought impossible to commingle; experience as 'aesthetic' depends on its being consummatory, drawing different dimensions together to occasion a lived experience that coordinates those dimensions towards a fruitful culmination.

How do our opening dining experiences stack up on this measure? The El Celler meal definitely manifests sophistication, talent and creativity. It clearly indicates ways in which the unlikely or seemingly impossible can be made possible. The kind of experience it engenders, though, is one mostly in line with the museum conception of art. The eater becomes a singular appreciator of the unfolding spectacle. The model for the 'aesthetic' experience remains that of onlookers who adopt a specific 'aesthetic' attitude to the scene that has been prepared just for them. Actually, onlookers, in the plural, may be an overstatement. The aesthetic situation can, in this case, be limited to spectacle and a solitary onlooker. Bracketing rather than amalgamation dominates. On the side of experience as lived event, the degree to which spectatorship dominates means that the combinatory elements are diminished. Also diminished is the degree to which the event is 'aesthetic'. Utility, the functional aspect, fades into the background, while beauty (manifested in the dessert by such qualities as innovation, surprise, representation) takes over the stage.

What about a meal manifesting Alice Waters's 'Delicious Revolution'? This one certainly has an aspect that recommends itself to what we are redefining as the 'aesthetic': combination. The functional aspect here is manifested by the inclusion of ethical concerns as important spillovers of how such meals are to be useful. In addition, the focus is on the experience as lived event. The experience is inseparable from a sensitivity to how the food is grown, considerations about values, attention to the pleasures of eating and the enhanced ability to appreciate the work of a talented chef because one has tried one's own hand at cooking.

So far, so good. Still, there remains one major question. What about artistry, fineness, in the actual cooking? Alice Waters could pull off fineness in her restaurant. Such a place, a critic could point out, is accessible only to those with a certain amount of disposable income. This, though, is not a major objection. Art and the wealth needed to support the highest levels of fineness have always gone together. Without papal patronage, the wonders of the Sistine Chapel ceiling would never have seen the light of day. To realize actual examples of the highest fineness will probably always involve patronage of some sort or other.

A more serious objection is whether the 'artistry' side of the Delicious Revolution will be emphasized. Reformers, especially those concerned with placing ethical issues front and centre, can readily slide into a kind of ascetic attitude, adopting a different separate-and-bracket practice of their own. The genre of jokes about vegetarians convincing themselves that lentil stew, tofu and other vegetarian staples are delicious tell the tale; in the presence of moral prescriptions, concerns about tastiness can be forced to the periphery. The temptation involves sliding into self-satisfied celebration of an experience heavy on the ethical dimension, but light on taste, beauty and the opportunity to push oneself to new levels of compossibility. Moral asceticism is always a temptation. Its suspicion of pleasure and beauty remains a constant danger that can upend the 'aesthetic' as we understand it.

The experience at a KFC in Ghana presents a good illustration of the fact that the aesthetic exists on a sliding scale and, furthermore, that it is the entire situation, not just a single art 'object' and single aesthetic 'subject', that is at issue. On the artistry side, there is little doubt that the KFC episode falls short. Fineness is fairly minimal. The food is formulaic, repeatable, capable of being prepared by relatively inexperienced hands. On the event-as-experience side, not much recommends itself either. Hardly anything is done to provide conditions that will have a good chance of enhancing the occurrence. The setting is predictable, not especially comfortable or conducive to shared, lengthy conversations. Everything indeed is designed for efficiency, speed of ingestion and quick departure to allow room for other customers.

In this case, what gives the experience real presence on the aesthetic scale are the elements present in the overall event: the challenging day, the difficulties of negotiating life in a strange place, the confusion about what to order in local restaurants, memories of home, the cool interior, a general sense of relaxation. In other words, the setting, scene and context as a whole offer a foothold into the aesthetic; situation, as we said earlier, matters. Something consummatory is being experienced. The aesthetic experience, minimal though it may be, is not missing entirely. When the stomach becomes a player in developing a philosophical take on things, sharp separations and neat exclusions become inappropriate. What we bring to an event can nonetheless contribute to the creation of a setting that offers some combination of beauty, utility, pleasure and goodness. In other words, eating at KFC *can* be an aesthetic experience.

When philosophy moves from the generative idea of a mind riding around in a bodily case to one that embraces the entire human being (in our terms, one that remembers the stomach), it is not surprising that the family of associated concepts will accordingly change their meanings. We have shown that situating the 'aesthetic' within the new setting necessarily moves its meaning away from what it connoted in a field dominated by the spectator approach. The previous field offered us a set of clear distinctions; that was its strong suit. Its weakness was that the distinctions had become hardened into rigid oppositions. Our approach has tried to recontextualize the making of distinctions without eliminating them altogether. We might not agree with Deresiewicz when he simply dismisses the notion that food can be art. We do agree with him, however, when he warns that 'if art is everything, then it is nothing.'[24] By highlighting the combination of setting, artistry and consummatory experience, by insisting on preserving fineness as a central ingredient and by replacing the on–off switch with a concept of continuity, we hope to have developed a fruitful alternative. Our alternative preserves what is best in the older model while reworking the meanings of art and the aesthetic in ways consistent with ordinary experience, true to the quest for excellence, open to non-Western artistry and welcoming of our status as hungry, cooking beings.

III

Tasting, Testing, Knowing

Knowing What is Good for Us

Eating can be an awfully complicated proposition. Suppose you're the grocery buyer for a family of four, living on a modest income in a major urban area with decent supermarkets. How do you decide on what to spend the family's weekly food budget? Should a hefty portion of it go towards purchasing fruits and vegetables? If so, should these be fresh, canned, frozen or some combination? Should you focus on 'organic' goods? Goods for which you have clipped coupons? What about the demands of the other members of your household? What do they like? What do they refuse to eat? What about the health risks of workers who harvest food: should you take into account their working conditions, the pay they earn, as you make your selections? If you make choices one way – say, free range meat and organic fresh vegetables – your grocery basket will most likely become filled with ultra-pricey commodities. Given the hefty portion of your budget taken up by these purchases, what will you leave out? Will you still be able to guarantee that your (growing, hungry) kids get enough food – literally, enough calories? Can you, aiming to reduce costs and get a better sense of where food comes from, perhaps grow a garden, make your own bread? Will you have time to do that with your full-time job and still spend time with your kids? And will those foods you purchase be grown by unionized workers or local cooperative growers whose farms you can inspect and whose philosophy you adhere to? (Perhaps you can get a day off work to go out and inspect that farm.)

It's a delicate balancing act. 'Just make the best-informed judgements you can', some well-meaning friend might suggest. Sounds good. Actually, it's one of those 'too good to be true' scenarios. If it's *information* about our food that we seek, it's available – in quantity. You probably could find out every single piece of information we've mentioned, about every single morsel of food you wish to put in your mouth. Gathering information about source, cost, relative nutritional value and their impact on other purchases might be helpful, but 'knowing about' all of these things still does not translate into 'knowing what to do', right now, on this shopping trip. A couple of problems present themselves: first of all, amassing information (being 'informed') isn't the same as knowing, and knowing is not the same as being wise. *Being* wise often requires finessing various trade-offs and compromises. Collecting more and more bits of data about our food does not necessarily enable us to generate a better, more complete, fuller answer to the question 'how are we to eat?'

Deciding what to eat can feel pretty daunting. The flood of (often scary) information can paralyse decision-making every bit as often as it can aid it. Thanks to a powerful combination of the Internet, vigorous alternative food movements and a well-oiled mainstream industrial food system, we in the West can know a tremendous amount about the candy bar or the peach, steak or energy drink we're about to put in our mouths. Correction: we can gather a tremendous amount of information, data, trivia, spin, advertising, gossip, opinion and so on, but whether or not that adds up to knowing anything about the food – and whether or not we then know 'how to eat' – are other matters altogether.

This chapter is an exploration of the question 'how do we know how we are to eat?' – a kind of nested question, or a question within a question, at one remove from the question 'how are we to eat?' itself. This means we are going to be dealing with epistemology, the name philosophers give to the study of the theory of knowledge. Our approach differs from inherited conceptions of epistemology in ways that result directly from our attending to food. When we take our stomach-y, mouth-y, feel-y, smell-y, busy-in-the-kitchen natures seriously, the answer to the question 'how do we know?' is quite different from the answer you get if you pretend that humans are bodiless Thinkers who stand at a glass wall's remove from the External World. As we undertake this examination, we will find ourselves digging deeper into – and becoming more sceptical about – some of the most fundamental and pervasive dichotomies shaping that history. We'll also begin to understand why Mary Midgley is right: 'applied philosophy' just won't *do* as a name for philosophizing that begins in everyday, stomach-endowed experience.[1] It suggests a faulty starting assumption: that there is on one hand theory or method and on the other hand some 'stuff' onto which that theory or method is applied, the way one might apply antiseptic to a wound. Food-related experiences and activities – cultivating, harvesting, cooking, eating – happen in situations that make it difficult to meaningfully separate theory from 'stuff' without doing violence to the situation.

Another change in our approach to epistemology disrupts the old hierarchy of the senses which privileges vision above all the others. As we noted in Chapter Two, our approach does not invert that hierarchy in some kind of simplistic 'taste above all other senses' move, but instead emphasizes the cooperation among the senses, a cooperation well exemplified by our actual experience of tasting, which tends to enlist all the senses, not just the sense involving the tongue. A bonus of this attention to taste is that it allows us to notice an etymological link between *tasters* and *testers*.

Indeed, the activity that will guide our investigation of knowing is just that: testing/tasting. The Latin name for our sub-species underscores that activity – doubly. Humans, it turns out, are not just *Homo sapiens*. We are, most technically, *Homo sapiens sapiens*, a name that – no kidding – acknowledges the centrality of food. While philosophers have often preferred 'rational' as a label for humans, a more literal translation of *sapiens* would identify us as the 'tasting species'.[2] *Sapiens* derives from the verb *sapere*, which means 'to think or discern' – or 'to taste or smell'. Etymology thus points at an answer to our question: how are we to eat? One answer – encoded in our very biological classification: experimentally, thoughtfully, wisely, judiciously. By tasting.

Facts and Values: Knowing is Valuing

The food mess with which the chapter begins bears all the hall-marks of a quintessential philosophy-as-plumbing problem. The mess catches us up and swamps us at several different levels. There's a set of empirical questions that need to be answered: how much does it cost? Who produced it? By what farming methods was it grown? Where does it come from? Will my household eat it? What is its nutritional profile? Does it taste good? But the answers to those empirical questions seem to rest on underlying commitments, paradigms or assumptions – ethical, aesthetic, environmental, health-related. At the very least, those commitments will require us to choose which empirical questions move front and centre, and which are present only peripherally. In addition, those commitments themselves often conflict; not only do different ethical priorities vie with each other to be 'most correct', but ethical commitments challenge environmental ones, environmental ones challenge aesthetic ones, and all can conflict with plain old taste – especially late at night, at the service station mini-mart, on the cross-country road trip, fifteen hours into the journey.

All of these commitments or paradigms can vie for supremacy and compete for territory. Which should rule over the others in one's life? A good household provider wants food that is healthy, tasty, filling, within range of a limited budget and provides some variety. (It is possible, as one food researcher put it, to focus on the health side, but 'How many dishes can you cook with potatoes and carrots before you say, "Kentucky Fried" is not so bad after all?'[3])

When we start paying careful attention to food messes, in the hope of using philosophy to sort them out, we begin to notice that their messiness derives in no small part from the fact that we don't know which concerns to prioritize – or even what it would mean to prioritize them. This is where the leaky pipes of the earlier epistemological plumbing start to cause problems. Earlier epistemologies set up ideal knowing conditions that were wonderful to behold, but had little to say to the perplexed shopper making apparently mundane decisions about groceries. Plato (*c.* 427–*c.* 347 BCE) got the 'wonderful to behold' ball rolling by insisting on a sharp distinction between 'knowledge' and 'opinion'. Descartes subsequently identified two key criteria for knowledge: it must be clear and it must be distinct. Kant insisted that real knowledge must be 'apodictic', that is, absolutely certain. Eventually, these epistemological exercises in neat separation led to a distinction (an unbridgeable chasm, really) between facts and values, formulated most prominently by David Hume (1711–1776). As a result of this separation, facts became the purview of objective knowledge. The realm of values came to be associated with subjective judgements.

Grocery shoppers challenge these sharp separations every time they deliberate over what to put in their basket; their puzzlement cannot be explained by appealing to a distinction between absolutely certain knowledge and mere opinion, or by reference to clarity and distinctness or – least of all – by drawing attention to some fundamental difference between fact and value. Shoppers' problems are partly problems about knowing, but – crucially – they are also partly questions about valuing; like most problems in life, it's complicated. These tomatoes are nutritious. Those free range eggs are expensive. This package of chicken is being sold on its expiration date; it is on sale. That chard is less expensive this week, but two members of the household refuse to eat chard. Cheetos are cheap and remarkably delicious. When we consider such ordinary-life observations – something academic philosophy typically fails to do – we become much less cavalier about sorting them out neatly into the two bins of fact and value. 'Tomatoes are nutritious' is both a factual statement and an evaluative one. Not only that, but neither its factual nor its evaluative dimensions stand alone. Other products are also nutritious, cost is a factor, meal planning is another, distaste by some household members is yet another. Desire for enjoyable, delicious, pleasurable meals is still another. Choosing foods to fill a grocery basket is, it turns out, incredibly complicated.

Such food messes also turn out to be very useful philosophically. They compel us to realize that we can only answer epistemological questions ('How can we *know* that we have answered the question "how should we eat?" correctly?') by taking very seriously the value dimensions of the question. Epistemology, we observe, always intersects with ethics and aesthetics. People in their everyday lives tend to live this conjunction quite matter-of-factly. For professional philosophers, it tends to be another matter entirely. Many of us tend to be tidy-minded types, bothered by intersecting and overlapping complexities.

Philosophers in the twentieth-century analytic tradition framed this opposition between facts and values (which philosophers call the 'fact–value distinction') as a matter of 'is' and 'ought', arguing that answers to the question 'what ought to be the case?' can never be derived from the answers to questions about what *is* the case. The so-called 'is–ought fallacy' held that 'ought' questions are different *in kind* from 'is' questions. Some kind of catastrophe results whenever we do not keep the questions rigorously separate. As is usual, this fallacy offers examples well suited to the position being defended. For instance, we cannot go from an observation such as 'pigs can feel pain and have a highly developed intelligence' ('is' statement) to claims such as 'pigs ought not be killed in front of each other' ('ought' statement). Analytic philosophers have tended to emphasize the gap in the direction from fact to value, insisting that you cannot derive moral claims from 'purely' epistemic ones.

One reason why many analytic philosophers have held that facts and values are fundamentally different is that they hold facts to be objective, the results of inquiries meeting appropriate standards of rationality. Values, on the other hand, are considered subjective, based on internal and individual preferences and not justifiable on the basis of standards. Objective claims are (typically) understood to be public, reproducible and a-perspectival. To assert that 'water boils at 100°C at sea level in ordinary pressure' is to make a claim that anyone (with the right equipment and in the right locale) can reproduce and observe. On the other hand, to say 'water from the New York City municipal water system tastes better than the water from any other public water source in the United States' is to make a claim that is relative to a particular taster – an aesthetic claim. One claim is person-specific; the other is generalizable – or so adherents to the dichotomy between fact and value would hold.

For many analytic philosophers the same scenario applies to moral issues: it is not simply aesthetic judgements that are subjective (matters of 'taste', as it were), but moral judgements, too. Ethicist Charles Stevenson (1908–1979) was willing to embrace this position to the fullest. He popularized a theory that came to be known as the 'boo/hurrah' theory of ethics. According to Stevenson, an assertion such as 'wasting water is bad' is simply an elaborate way of saying: 'water wasting! Boo!' That is, in using the word 'bad', you are simply encouraging someone else to think (and act) as you do. You're 'cheerleading' for a particular position. There are no reasons to which you can (ultimately) appeal, no justification you can give, to provide a warrant for your moral claim. If the tidy-minded categorizations apply – if ethical claims are subjective, and if 'subjective' means 'about the perceiver' – what other result could there be? Ought from is? Boo! Is–ought dichotomy? Hurrah!

As mentioned earlier, the great precursor of this position was David Hume. His more formal description draws the distinction between 'feelings' or 'sentiments' (which he associated with the heart) and 'speculation' or 'affirmation' (associated with the head).[4] Heaven forbid that a philosopher would admit to a heart-and-head team, no matter how effectively such a team works in the grocery store.

As we have emphasized already, attentive (an adjective chosen to evoke the tactility of 'tender' and 'tending') consideration of our relationships to food reveals the inadequacy and inaccuracy of time-worn dichotomies like objective/subjective, mind/body and theoretical/practical. The fact/value distinction is similarly limited. Food-making activities and the relationships they manifest are most usefully (and fruitfully, creatively, constructively) understood in terms of context; of imbrication, interrelationship and interpenetration; of mutual influence. Facts *are* always value laden. They don't just pop up out of nowhere, having nothing to do with ongoing activities and concerns. And, by the way, values are always 'fact laden'. They are not devoid of attention to detail, to consequences. We can, of course, always artificially limit what we mean. We can stipulate, in a particular context, that the 'facts' we are considering *must* be 'value free', but this will have everything to do with seeking a safe haven retreat for the tidy-minded types (an admitted temptation for professional philosophers) and little to do with ordinary ways of engaging in everyday practices.

Lisa once found a very large, beautiful and very fresh-looking mushroom growing in a field. A neighbour reported that he was 'pretty sure' it was a meadow mushroom, or one of its relatives. He listed a few of the characteristics that were apparently 'dead giveaways', so to speak. Perhaps, before actually ingesting it, he suggested, another neighbour should be consulted. That neighbour was a retired mycology professor who lived just down the road. A quick consult in his driveway revealed that the mushroom was indeed edible – maybe a horse mushroom, maybe a meadow mushroom, definitely an edible mushroom. He was quietly confident, firm. He explained how to distinguish this particular fungus from the vaguely similar, ominously named 'destroying angel' mushroom (highly poisonous). His recommendation: 'treat it like a Portobello.'

Scientific knowledge had spoken through this man; the mushroom was safe to eat. Pictures of it were emailed to friends, along with descriptions of plans for its preparation. Fried with a lump of good butter in a hot cast iron pan, it was delicious. Still, the entire experience was a bit frightening. When, at night, a small, momentary gut cramp made itself felt, there was panic – just for a moment. 'Yes, it was delicious, but was it tasty enough to die for?'[5]

Such a story, in its detail, is revealing for emphasizing the degree to which eating reduces the gap between us and the rest of the world. It shows how eating changes both us and the thing eaten – an experience that can be glorious but can also be deeply unnerving when one has insufficient information. And, here's the rub that takes us away from the dream world of tidy-minded philosophers: one *never* has perfect, absolutely certain information to warrant putting something in one's mouth. We can never reduce to zero the chance that our encounter with this foodstuff will be unhappy. In the case of mushrooms, for instance, even the experts can be wrong; mushroomers love to recount the famous (and tragic) story of a mycology professor who accidentally ate a poisonous mushroom and died. A more likely, less dramatic result is that, ten years hence, some food we now regularly eat *because* it is healthful will be declared harmful. Indeed, this is just the fate experienced by the poor chicken egg seemingly about once per decade. But eat we must, and in doing so, we must make ourselves vulnerable in a way that is nearly unique, even among bodily experiences. It's not that it is the most dangerous thing we humans routinely do (driving probably has that distinction for those of us in car cultures); it's that it's absolutely one of the most intimate things we do, and its intimacy is what makes danger possible.

Eating, if it serves as an analogy for, or literal form of, inquiry does so by reminding us of our vulnerability as inquirers – or, if you like, of our porousness. It encourages us to see inquiry not as a path undertaken by an 'objective' – detached, indifferent – observer that leads to clear, certain, unambiguous knowledge. Rather, it encourages conceiving inquiry as an ongoing activity that calls us to risk, to be open and to learn to act with less certainty than we would like.

'This mushroom is edible' offers a good entry to thinking about human knowing in general. It also indicates, in an important way, how fact and value intertwine. The mushroom's edibility can't be neatly parcelled out as a fact without significant implications, nor as a merely subjective imposition on a neutral material. This is because humans, *qua* humans, are *interested*, invested and – most of all – needy. When we ask 'how are we to eat?' we are not asking the question from a perch outside the give-and-take of everyday life, and certainly not from a perch disconnected from the living of an individual life. Stomachs keep us involved – *invested* – in our surroundings, and those surroundings can respond in crucial ways to our needs. When we attend to facts, as well as to other aspects of knowing such as methods of inquiry and explanatory hypotheses, we are responding to our neediness, our curiosity, our investment in outcomes – in short, to the things we *value*.

Aristotle may have been right to proclaim that all humans desire to know. Philosophers have typically paid attention only to the 'know' aspect of this assertion, but have neglected the 'desire'. Knowing grows out of *valuing* ('desire') and returns to it again. Our relationships to food help us understand, with exceptional power, how clumsily inaccurate it is to treat knowing and valuing as activities that must be kept separate and distinct. The prosaic way in which food relationships manifest the intertwining of fact with aesthetic and ethical values is precisely what gives food-making relationships their illustrative power.

By purposely ignoring the stomach and its activities, our inherited philosophy too often sought its models for knowledge among the human activities that were exemplary in terms of clarity and certitude. Such models could be identified, but (and this side of things was not widely admitted) were unusual and atypical when it came to human life in general. Admittedly, the atypical cases were easier to work with; they allowed philosophers to keep away from more messy, more difficult to deal with situations. They provided solid, decisive results. But those are not reasons why they should be selected as *the* 'aspirational' sciences – models of what human inquiry in general should be.

We've had astronomy, geometry and physics held up as the illustrations of how we ought to go about thinking. The impetus may be sound – we've sought to advance human inquiry by choosing a domain of it that really seems to be making great achievements – but there's a danger in assuming that these fields' properties can be replicated in other fields. Descartes, as we have seen, selected geometry as his aspirational form of knowing. All forms of knowing that desire to be 'real' knowing must then approximate the ideal of geometry. Its unusual properties are taken as exemplary.

Geometry, it must be admitted, does offer special properties that appeal to the tidy-minded. At the same time, it's not very useful as the singular illustration of how knowledge works. Likewise, while we may be able to find an example of a domain of facts that are unrelated to values, such facts are going to be interesting because they are *unusual*, not because they illustrate the 'real' way facts and values (don't) relate. We need to resist the urge to take the unusual for the aspirational – a dangerous temptation for philosophers. Highlighting our status as hungry minimizes that temptation.

If you ask someone, entirely out of context, 'how are we to eat?', for instance, in reply you are likely to get a set of questions that boil down to this: what are you really asking, in asking such a question? What kind of *how* question is that; for *what purpose* are you asking it? Are you trying to preserve some ethical principles? To observe some religious precepts? To achieve some aesthetic goals; maintain some economic standards; promote some health requirements? The answer to the question 'how?' – an empirical question on the face of it – will always be 'it depends on what you are trying to do.' That, in turn, trades on the matter of what you think is valuable to be doing right now.

Ordinary language provides multiple examples of the weaving together of factual and evaluative dimensions. 'Dinner was late' is a claim that combines description (the serving of dinner in relation to clock time) and evaluation (the unpleasant dining experience that resulted). Once that serving is situated in the context of a particular project, the *fact* of late service cannot be separated neatly from the evaluative *consequence*. Words such as 'rotten', 'stale' or 'fresh' provide other examples. They indicate how descriptive characteristics blend readily into evaluative ones. If someone asks: 'How was the restaurant you tried last night?' and the answer is: 'It turned out to be an "all you can eat" kind of place', that response is, strictly speaking, describing a fact. At the same time it is an evaluative response, shorthand for 'it was not very flavourful or high-quality, but definitely a place you don't leave hungry.' Philosophy ought to recognize and seek to understand such ordinary ways of speaking – not discount them as confused ways of speaking.

When we turn aside from a dream world modelled on purity, certitude and perfect knowing, we can embrace our situatedness in a real world, where people need to eat. Instead of setting up purified, neat, clear deductive examples, we begin with situations likely to be encountered. Those typically involve three intersecting factors: the need to act (how should I fill up my shopping cart?); some time constraints (this has to be done during the next hour); and less-than-deductively-certain conclusions (can I be certain that choosing organic, more expensive carrots is the better choice?). *Necessity, time constraints, uncertainty*: these are the common factors of most situations we encounter. Determinations about what is best emerge from (i) the situation, (ii) the triple preconditions of *time, necessity, uncertainty,* (iii) the available ingredients and (iv) the meal envisioned. An epistemology can get no better start than by admitting such interconnections.

The Hierarchy of the Senses

Seeing is believing. 'Does he taste funny to you?' says one cannibal to another other as they devour a clown. All human-flesh-eating jokes aside, determining whether something you have just put into your mouth tastes the way it should or 'tastes funny' is an assessment of no small importance. Sometimes the question is a matter of preference: is the soup too salty? Does the salad need more garlic? Has the yoghurt fermented for long enough? Perhaps the question raises the spectre that our ethical, religious or other precepts are being violated: 'Does this smell like pork to you?' 'Is this mock duck or is it real duck, because it sure *feels* real in my mouth'. At other times, the question voices a health or safety concern: has the milk gone off? Is there wheat in this dish? Sometimes, the question is of literal life-or-death importance: 'Did you have peanut butter on this knife?' 'Do I smell shrimp?' 'Do you *really* know how to identify mushrooms?' *Practically* speaking, we rely on our tongues in concert with our noses (in particular) and our eyes to help us 'know' things – we do it all the time, in fact.

Philosophically speaking, not so much. As discussed in Chapter Two, we have inherited a hierarchy of the senses on which the proximate ones (taste, touch and, problematically, smell) are considered unreliable sources of, or conduits for, genuine knowledge. Reliable knowing is the preserve of the distal senses, sight and hearing. These are said to admit of greater objectivity because, among other things, they do not require us to touch the thing in question. Kant said that the proximate and the distal differ in terms of whether the sense experience draws us most to the thing itself or to our own sense; only the latter can bring objectivity.[6] To the degree to which the senses can provide us with knowledge at all, only specific ones can be counted upon to provide us with genuine knowledge. The others lead us – and here comes the neat Platonic knowledge/opinion separation – into the realm of mere opinion.

Were we to pay attention to ordinary language, we would find plenty of expressions in which English, at least, is richly interlarded with figures of speech that associate thinking, exchanging ideas and similar activities with eating. Such figures of speech tend to bring our attention to the fact that ideas really *do* become a part of us, and do so in ways that can be scary, uncomfortable, upsetting or otherwise problematic, the same way that it can be scary to ingest food. We speak, for instance, of an idea being 'difficult to swallow'; of someone gullible falling for an idea (like a fish) 'hook, line and sinker'. You might say that an idea 'sticks in your craw' – 'craw' being another name for the crop of a bird – the pouch on the oesophagus where food can be stored before going on to be digested. We have to 'chew over' ideas to make them more 'palatable' or 'easier to swallow' – and we often 'chew the fat' with friends. We 'can't stomach' upsetting ideas, meaning that we may literally 'lose our cookies' (vomit) if we think about them. We describe something we dislike or aren't interested in as 'not our cup of tea'; on the other hand, appealing ideas can 'go down well'. If in doubt about something's 'palatability', we may 'sugar-coat' it to ensure more ready ingestion.

Clearly, a rich assortment of expressions that use eating to describe thinking exists. For most Western philosophers, though, seeing dominates the discourse about inquiry. Philosophers have often used visual metaphors to illustrate the acquisition of knowledge, and their ways of speaking have come to be woven into vernacular expressions and idioms – think, for example, of how often you have said 'I see what you mean.'

Using vision as the defining sense is not an innocent, neutral move. It builds several features into a conception of knowing. Vision does not require one to get close to the object of inquiry; indeed, vision ceases to operate well when one *does* get too close to an object. We can't see something on the end of our nose, and we certainly can't see something inside our own mouth. By contrast, we can see things very clearly from some distance away, even if they are out of reach behind a plate-glass wall. We can keep the world at arm's length and not disrupt its operations. Such disconnection allows us to reflect objectively upon it. Based on its successes within certain scientific fields, we might even praise the 'behind the glass' approach as the ideal model for all knowing. Such a distance-privileging model also provides justification for a particular attitude towards the world: one of manipulation and domination, a connection that may seem counterintuitive on its face.

Plato famously offered a string of visual metaphors in Book VII of the *Republic* to illustrate the relationships between wisdom and knowledge, and reality and appearance. They include a cave, a fire, the sun and a divided line. In Plato's epistemology, *seeing clearly* is so powerful a metaphor for knowing that it almost ceases to be metaphorical. The details of his complex and rich allegories are not important to us here; the important thing to note about them is that, centuries before the rise of modern philosophy, vision already stood in for knowledge.

Vision-induced detachment went hand in hand with the type of science that emerged in the sixteenth century, a science that considered the natural world to be a kind of machine. What resulted was an important moral conjunction (the fact/value mix again). Set against an 'external' world made up of 'objects' understood in mechanistic terms, the newly self-defined 'subjects' were liberated in an important way: they could envision their task as being to manipulate, dominate, control or change those objects in the service of their own ends. Nothing in an 'object' or a 'machine' calls on an observer to 'have some respect for what I am'. Rather, objects and machines are, by definition, things to be manipulated; they are objects-*for*-a-subject, available for use and transformation. The detached spectator-subjects are now free to understand themselves as the only sources of value in the world. The fact/value distinction is born, a distinction which, we can now appreciate, is not neutral, does not *itself* respect the fact/value distinction. Rather, it opens and makes available justifications for unlimited transformation of the object-world.

During the twentieth century, there was a bit of push-back. We find, for example, a work published in 1989 with the title *The View from Nowhere*,[7] a phrase that takes the notion of an 'undistorted vantage point' to its logical, if impossible, conclusion. It expresses a desire for the kind of objectivity philosophers had long sought – dispassionate, disinterested, disengaged – and had sought to describe through the medium of vision. But the notion of a 'view' from *nowhere* pushes that juxtaposition of disengagement and vision to the point of absurdity, thereby revealing an unavoidable fact about vision. Distanc*ing* though that sense is, it nevertheless necessitates distanc*es*. Only bodies can be at physical distances from each other; we bodies are never 'nowhere'. We are always somewhere, somewhere with a particular (even if generalizable) vantage point. Not only that: the 'somewhere' is usually populated by other entities, and these are not best described as 'objects'.

Our stomach-friendly approach, in contrast, does not succumb either to the philosophical temptation to escape from the everyday world of nitty gritty detail to a purified realm, nor does it make us something we are not – spectators standing outside the push and pull of events. We admit where and what we are: engaged creatures involved in multiple dealings with our circumstances. This kind of approach discourages thinking of ourselves as epistemological subjects or of the world as made up of neutral, value-free objects towards which we have obligations only by choice. It also challenges the imperialism of vision, encouraging a combinatory understanding of how the senses work in relation to knowing.

Inquiry, testing, tasting. It's hard to be neutral with a slug in your mouth. Imagine this scene: a shopper buys a small container of golden cherry tomatoes at a farmer's market. She begins munching on the delicious fruit. Popping one into her mouth she becomes aware of a squishy, soft thing on its surface. She reacts instinctively, using a finger to flick it off the tomato and cleanly out of her mouth, somehow miraculously avoiding contact with her tongue, before vague awareness becomes specific recognition:

'Slug! Yuck!' The philosophical lesson: if we conceive of inquiry using metaphors of taste and touch (in addition to vision) we come to some dramatically different ways of thinking about the fundamentals of knowing. Using tasting as the sensory metaphor for inquiry suggests an activity characterized first by interest, not detachment (something that can, of course, be true of vision as well, but is not why that sense was prized). On a literal level, to taste something is either to be attracted to it or to struggle to overcome some level of aversion to it; it's hard even to imagine being neutral about something (food or anything else) going in your mouth. The pleasure or the aversion may be slight, but indifference is hard to imagine, or even to feign. Even using one's teeth to nip a stray thread from one's sleeve brings with it a reaction, however slight.

Understanding inquiry through tasting also suggests an *inescapable* intimacy between knower and known – a physical commingling that challenges received views about the inter-reliance between objectivity, dispassion and distance. Taking something into our mouths – or at least onto our tongues – is *the only* way we can ever taste it. Getting beyond the plate-glass window of detachment becomes not a mistake (as it is on vision-centred models) but an important component of inquiry, a component that presents itself as obvious when we leave behind the (idealized) model of the mathematician's whiteboard, the astronomy observatory or the physics laboratory and consider how anthropologists, psychologists, ethologists, volcanologists and entomologists – indeed, how most scientists of all sorts – carry out their work.

Finally, and most obviously, thinking about inquiry via tasting shifts our attention from the (disembodied) mind or even the (utterly embodied) brain as the seat of all knowing. It invites us to experience our entire bodies as inquiring, investigating, analysing entities. Our tongues do not function as 'instruments' of our minds when we taste, nor do they taste 'all by themselves'. Tasting happens when tongue, nose, brain, teeth, lips – even fingers, ears and, of course, eyes collaborate to converge on a foodstuff and take it in. 'Taking it in' is a useful phrase to describe such a process, and it functions both literally and metaphorically to describe it thus. To begin the process of tasting something, we might 'take it in' with our eyes and (in many instances) nose; we look at and smell it. If the thing *looks* repulsive (for example, if it is covered with a material such as mould, which we have come to associate with danger or at least with distaste; or if it looks very like the animal that it once was, and is curled in what appears to be an agonized contortion) we might be put off by it – or we might not be.[8] If it *smells* fetid or putrid (think of durian, the fruit banned from lifts and aeroplanes in many parts of South and Southeast Asia, or brick cheese, the smelliest cheese to come out of Wisconsin), we might be still more put off. Taking something in with one's nose feels, and quite literally *is*, more intrusive than taking it in with one's eyes. We can shut our eyes without damage to our organism but we cannot shut down our noses without affecting respiration, which would obviously be harmful for us. While both senses might be defined as 'distal', smells nonetheless get 'taken in' by us in a rather more material way than do sights. We might close our eyes and still 'see' the green mould on the cheese, but in the case of a challenging smell, the molecules producing that smell literally linger in our noses even after we walk away from the smelly object. If we're allergic, those mould spores can have enough contact with us to trigger a reaction.

Touch is often the next sense enlisted, as we pick up the object with our fingers, or perhaps through our finger extensions – a fork, a spoon, chopsticks. Is the food slippery? Rough? Malleable? In many Western societies, we are discouraged from doing much 'testing' of food with our fingers; we teach children early on not to 'play with their food' because we consider it rude, messy, unruly. As we mature, we can come to feel our food virtually, through those finger extensions known as eating utensils – if we're paying attention, that is, which we *are* most often when the texture is unexpected (a too-hard potato in the salad, mushy pasta, a tough-to-cut piece of meat). But whether or not our fingers are enlisted, touch is nevertheless definitely at work when a food enters our mouth; the tongue tends to be a far more sensitive organ of touch than is the fingertip anyway. Unctuous, crisp, brittle, grainy; such concepts make up the 'mouthfeel' of a food. In food tasting, the term 'mouthfeel' refers to the touch of a food on one's tongue, and also the sensation of it on one's lips, teeth and the insides of the cheeks.

At this point, you have *taken in* the food in a very literal sense; it has come to be inside you unlike any visual image can ever be. It is on its way to becoming you in a cellular sense. The chances are good that as your tongue and teeth encounter a foodstuff, it will give off a sound, which will be carried to you through the bones of your head as much as through your (external) ears; a crunch (a potato chip or crispy, fried cricket), a soft squirt (an orange segment or juice-filled piece of chewing gum), a liquidy slurp (a soft drink or the fermentation juices collecting in a pot of pickles). Sounds may not come to the forefront of one's consciousness while eating, but, again, their absence or unusualness can indicate, subtly and sotto voce, that something is not right: the potato chip doesn't crunch but 'sogs'; the orange doesn't squirt, it breaks drily. It can also indicate that things are supremely right: a 'proper' baguette makes a very characteristic sound when it is torn in half. If the sound is absent, it is simply not a proper baguette.

After all this, literal tasting – the thing taste buds do in isolation – is really rather anticlimactic. The thing we call 'tasting' is of course an activity of both tongue and nose; plug your nose and you will dramatically reduce the wallop of that sauerkraut in your mouth. But less noted is the fact that were we simply to encounter, say, chocolate as a sensation on the tongue (or even on the tongue and in the nose), it would not be nearly the pleasurable experience it is when we enlist all the senses we have. Thus when we speak of tasting here, we should always be understood to mean this collaborative activity. Indeed, one of the strengths of using the sense of taste as a metaphor and model for knowing is the fact that it can remind us (better than vision can) not to isolate the senses from each other, as if each could carry on its work alone.

With familiar foods, sensory experiences can tell us that things are 'normal' (the potato chips are fresh and crispy) or 'extraordinary' (really great chocolate!) or 'wrong' (this milk is spoiled). When a food is unfamiliar, we often rely on more than one feature of our experience to confirm our sense that things are 'off'. Whereas, for example, I usually want to taste milk that smells as if it might be going off (because the combination of smelling and tasting will determine far more conclusively than smell alone whether milk is still drinkable), or I might put a piece of cheese in my mouth to see if the mould that had visibly covered its surface has also imparted an unwelcome flavour, in the case of unfamiliar foods we are somewhat at sea. Is it *supposed* to feel rubbery in our mouths? To smell like old gym socks? To look like it's wearing a fur coat? Does this flavour mean it's spoiled, or is this what it tastes like when it's ripe? Durian is notorious for smelling like a very-long-dead thing that wasn't edible in the first place; its luscious flavour doesn't at all 'match' its stink. The same is true for many mild cheeses that smell like a concentration of dirty gym socks – Limburger, for instance. Tasting the unfamiliar involves careful probing, but also, likely, some quizzing of others more experienced with the food.[9]

Carolyn Korsmeyer, whose aesthetic theory was discussed in Chapter Two, refers to this interrelationship among the senses as 'communion', 'collaboration' and 'synaesthesia' (Korsmeyer and others use the last term in a somewhat informal sense rather than in its strictest technical sense). She illustrates the intertwining of the senses when we eat in ways that require one to rethink some traditional prejudices. Perhaps you have heard the story of a taste test in which people were told they were drinking red wine when in fact they were drinking white, and you have thought, 'Aha! I *knew* those snobs couldn't tell the difference!' The presupposition lurking behind the 'Aha!' moment is that one *should* be able to identify, on the basis of taste (and smell) alone, what one is tasting – be it red wine or white, fresh shrimp or aquarium cleanings, cheese or the contents of a compost bin. But as those wry examples, extended from her text, suggest, tasting is coupled to other senses, especially (for sighted persons) vision. We can experience as foul something that, were we to be given enough other sensory context, we would actually find extremely pleasant. Korsmeyer cites an experiment in which people were unable to eat faeces-shaped chocolate, even if they could smell that it was chocolate. A visual message is sometimes so strong that it cannot be overcome.[10] In contrast, once she realized her husband had put shrimp in the salad she was eating, the taste of 'low tide' she had experienced on the first bite immediately dissipated, and the foul taste became desirable. (One of us finds that with her eyes closed the smell of her compost bucket is irresistible, like that of a wonderful cheese.)

The use of taste – this multifaceted experience – as an appropriate metaphor for inquiry has been embraced by the anthropologist David Sutton. He has even invented a word to describe the position: 'I suggest the term *gustemology*, a gustemic way of knowing, living and interacting'.[11] He writes that 'in a gustemological approach, taste takes on the quality of a total social fact, tied to multiple domains of social life'; the approach recognizes 'that our experience of food (like all of life) is always inherently synesthetic'.[12]

Modern humans, to use our full taxonomic label, are *Homo sapiens sapiens*. That second *sapiens* indicates our subspecies and distinguishes us (should we ever need to be so distinguished) from other known *Homo sapiens* subspecies, now extinct. On other taxonomic systems, we are simply *Homo sapiens*, a name that is generally translated as 'wise man'. Presumably, this suggests that our subspecies name means 'wise, wise man'. A nice pat on the back, but perhaps an even better one would come from the more literal translation: 'tasters'. *Sapiens*, as mentioned earlier, derives from the verb *sapere*, which does indeed mean 'to discern', 'to think' or 'to understand'. But, notably, this definition stands alongside two others: 'to sense' and, very specifically, 'to taste'. Depending on the dictionary you consult, one or more of these definitions might even appear *before* 'to think or discern'. While it is unlikely that the great classifier Linnaeus actually intended for our species to be named 'the tasters', the ancient Latin connection between tasting and discerning, thinking and understanding is ineradicably encoded in this etymology. If we conceive of inquiry through the experience of tasting, we are led to think about inquiry as experimentation or testing. Inquiry-as-tasting/ testing would be anything but 'hands off'. One could hardly conceive of a form of interaction with the 'external' world that leaves one more entangled with it.

The contrasts between knowing-as-tasting and knowing-as-seeing are significant. First and most fundamentally, tasting acknowledges our 'porousness', our interactive relationships with other organisms. That, in turn, causes us to notice that we are fundamentally engaged in doings and undergoings with things. We are not primarily knowers. Knowing is but one aspect of how we come to grips with the world in which we live.

Second, tasting cannot happen from a neutral standpoint (the taste from nowhere?) but always happens in a place that is supremely, manifestly involved and interested (within, and in the vicinity of, one's body). That doesn't mean, however, that it is necessarily utterly subjective – that is, capricious and therefore utterly random. We recognize various ways in which one can cleanse (in an immediate way) and educate (in a long-term way) one's palate. Some tastes do send a signal, such as 'this food is dangerous' or 'this requires an educated palate.' It can be true that 'this food is dangerous *for me*', but the addition of 'for me' does not make the matter one of mere subjective opinion. It is not that the individual says 'I perform an act of will that declares that this foodstuff be dangerous'; rather, the interactions between ingested material and physiology run their own course, regardless of what acts of will accompany it. This seeming paradox of subjectivity/

objectivity ('this is dangerous' really means 'this is dangerous *for me*') is paradoxical only when we come to the table toting a pre-disposition to believe that reliable knowledge requires dispassion, distance, universality, neutrality and a setting that is contextless.

Third, tasting draws upon our entire person – all senses, our emotional capacities, our memory – in undertaking its work.[13] Our assessments of taste ('that's chocolate' or 'that's disgusting') will be shaped by the degree to which these various faculties are working (together) and the degree to which we are (able to be) attentive to them. (Swamp or shrimp?)

Fourth, tasting errors are of a sort different from errors of vision. Attending to them would lead us to come up with categories different from 'knowledge' and 'opinion'. How would Descartes' first Meditation have read had he grounded his uncertainty and doubt in questions about things he tasted, rather than things he saw? Surely his neat descent into general scepticism, 'I can doubt everything', would have been tempered. Instead of worrying about the absence of perfect certitude, he would have been encouraged to keep testing. After all, remaining a sceptic about food is kind of life threatening. Overall, his position, filtered through the category of taste, would end up being modified. The claim 'everything can be doubted' makes for good copy and public relations, but the more attenuated 'we have to build on what we know and inquire about what remains uncertain' would have been a more likely outcome, had he started with taste.

Objectivity. The spectre of objectivity has been haunting this chapter. It is time to take it on directly. Tasting has notoriously been described as the sense that will not admit of objectivity. There's no accounting for taste, we are told regularly. Taste (so David Hume tells us) is subjective, which, within one school of Western philosophy, means exclusively personal, idiosyncratic – not at all associated with judgements that are 'objective', a term understood in that school to be associated with neutral data universally available to everyone in the same way. Furthermore, the interrelationships among the senses that contribute to our ordinary experience of tasting are pointed to as evidence of the inferiority of taste as an objective sense. That is, if we find we cannot taste the chocolate as delicious because we can *see* that it is shaped like faeces, doesn't this indicate that taste is unreliable? So (the argument continues), not only is taste subjective (varying dramatically among eaters), it is also influenced by factors 'unrelated' to it, such as appearance and texture. These claims have added up to the argument that taste (and other proximate senses, but especially taste) is subjective: capricious, idiosyncratic and an imposition of one's prejudices onto a subject-matter. There's no building objective (pure, unbiased, neutral) knowledge upon it.

But consider this: it *does* make sense to argue about whether the loaf of sandwich bread that lasts a week on the shelf is better than one just out of the oven, or whether one brand of ice cream or one winemaker's product tastes better than another. If these are issues worth discussing, then perhaps the best description of the situation is not one that highlights the label 'purely subjective'. For 'subjective' in this sense would mean: it's just my choice and that's all it is. The categories of better and worse choice, as well as the reasons they might be better or worse, simply would not apply.

Ordinary experience suggests that an alternative position, one that admits judgements of quality along with intelligent discussions about them, makes perfect sense when it comes to taste. How can this be? For philosophers caught up in the sharp fact/value split, or subjective/objective dichotomy, this has been a difficult puzzle. How to save both ordinary ways of speaking and inherited philosophical presuppositions? David Hume offers one good example in his essay 'Of the Standard of Taste'. He argues, in effect, that taste (including aesthetic taste) *is* subjective. He goes on, however, to add an important qualifier: we-the-perceivers *create and reinforce* standards that 'do business as' objectivity. For Hume, we act 'as if' there were some kind of objectivity even though we 'know' there isn't. This 'as if' strategy is about as good as it gets when it comes to the objectivity of taste – at least, if one remains committed to typical assumptions and standards centred on humans as detached spectators.

A stomach-endowed take on things need not remain committed to such assumptions. Indeed, it suggests something very different: namely, that we humans are continually engaged in coming to grips with our surroundings. We are *invested* in coming to grips with them; it matters to us, sometimes in a life-or-death way. This feature of human be-ing orients and shapes all our activity, including inquiry and knowing, which can never be regarded as dispassionate, disengaged activities. Thus, our model of inquiry acknowledges interconnectedness among our senses, our sensations and our emotional states. It understands influences such as hunger, loud noises or worries about pesticide residue not as 'distortions' to be filtered out of the knowing process but as features of ourselves and our surroundings with which we must come to grips.

Such a model of inquiry also requires a conception of objectivity that does not rest upon a sharp distinction between the self and the world, or emphasize disinterestedness, dispassion and disconnectedness. Our model of objectivity begins at the mouth and focuses instead on responsiveness, along with its related notion, responsibility. In some traditions of Buddhism, there is a notion of *skilfulness*, used instead of moral concepts such as 'good', to describe the kind of behaviour a human being ought to cultivate. We suggest borrowing this notion for epistemological purposes, to serve as a basis for reworking the notion of objectivity. Objectivity, understood as appropriate, skilful responsiveness to a context, would begin from an acknowledgement of one's situatedness in the world: 'there's a slug in my mouth' versus 'I occupy the view from nowhere'. In a paper written with Stephen Kellert in 1995, one of us (Lisa Heldke) developed a view of objectivity *as* responsibility, which defines objective inquiry as that which acknowledges, fulfils and expands the framework of investigation among participants in the endeavour – where 'participants' include not just 'knowers' but 'the known'.[14]

How can this notion preserve what was best in the older notion of objectivity? It builds on a robust acknowledgement of the fact that, when understood as an adequate grasp of things, objectivity does not operate with an on–off switch. We do not get a perfect image of an object in the mind-considered-as-mirror. Rather, as engaged and interested participants, we keep responding to our situations in ways that can be tinkered with and made more adequate in light of various objectives we have in view. We can enhance our ways of approaching these objectives; that is, we can improve the objectivity of our accounts, over time. 'Getting it right' is indeed a feature of the traditional notion of objectivity that needs to be preserved. But whereas the traditional notion emphasizes fixedness and finality, our alternative stresses the provisional, situational and always-reassessing quality of inquiry, and indeed of objectivity itself. Such a notion well serves the understanding of humans as active beings, invested in 'dealing' with our surroundings.

Readers can now get a sense of how the conception of objectivity as responsibility intersects with the notion of inquiry built around the conjunction of senses, rather than on the single model of vision. It offers a comprehensive alternative to the hierarchy embedded in the proximal/distal relationship. Response – responsibility – is always relational. Considered relationally, there is no unique or special value associated with distance *alone*, even while there might be plenty of circumstances in which emphasizing distance for specific purposes is appropriate. But if objectivity is a function of acknowledging and fulfilling the bonds of our relationships, then senses that emphasize relationality come to have their own kind of special properties and values. Such an emphasis on relationality also discourages the sharp opposition between subjectivity and objectivity. Such a sharp opposition can emerge only within the general framework of a mind-centred philosophy. A focus on relationality and responsibility encourages that attention be paid to 'between-ness' rather than the 'about me-ness versus the about the object-ness' that characterizes traditional concepts of subjectivity and objectivity.

Why Food?

We are now in a position to bring together the various strands of our inquiry. We will do this by making explicit how food, food-making and eating can contribute to epistemology, now defined as a way of coming to grips with processes of inquiry.

To be clear, we do not mean to offer our account of food, philosophy and their intertwining as the only forms of human experiencing on which philosophers should draw. Rather, we are pointing to the ways in which traditional philosophy's purposeful excision of all such activities has led to a distorted understanding of who we are. This distortion has led, in turn, to distorted notions of knowing and inquiry. The philosophical value of food – and, in the context of this chapter, the epistemological significance of food-making and eating – emerge instead from their centrality in human life, from their necessity for human life and from the multiple layers of meaning these activities can take on and accommodate. In making this claim, we are using a definition of inquiry that owes much to the thought of John Dewey, who wrote that 'Inquiry is the controlled or directed transformation of an indeterminate situation into one that is so determinate in its constituent distinctions and relations as to convert the elements of the original situation into a unified whole.'[15]

The position from which we begin is one that should need no emphasizing: humans must eat or somehow take in nutrients.[16] This makes eating one of a remarkably short list of 'vitals' without which human life cannot be sustained. That list also contains sleep, shelter, clothing and eliminating. Eating, like sleeping, clothing and sheltering, is an activity we engage in not only out of necessity, but also for recreation, pleasure, religious and cultural observation, and many other reasons that remind us that we are 'hungry beings' who like to enjoy and celebrate life. Notably, sleeping and eliminating bodily waste tend not to be such activities; 'sleeping together' doesn't describe a literal activity the way that 'eating together' does. And while some cultures do have a practice that could be described as 'social defecation', it can hardly compare to the elaborate and multifaceted ways in which eating is a cultural activity. So, eating is on a (relatively short) list of vitally important human needs that lends itself to being embroidered and elaborated in countless ways.

Recognizing this and emphasizing the fact that humans are not detached spectators but engaged participants, food-making activities present us with rich examples of what we call 'thoughtful practices'. Again, food-making activities are anything but unique as thoughtful practices, but they do provide vivid examples. In their vividness, they point out just how important to human beings is this category of activities. The expression 'thoughtful practices' is meant to capture several qualities which we discussed above. It calls us to conjunctions rather than to the more typical exclusive disjunctions emphasized by philosophies that ignore the stomach. Notice that practising is, itself, a reflective activity: it does not just engage your 'mind' or 'brain' but engages your entire person. You think and reflect with/through/in your hands, your arms and calf muscles when you bake bread or cultivate crops. Thinking and practising are not two separate activities, one bodily and one 'mental'. Furthermore and of a piece with that, we notice that thinking is not purely mental or solely connected with the brain – a claim that will shock philosophers of a certain kind. Thinking is itself a practice – a practice that can tire us out, that requires us to take sustenance, that can go better or worse depending on the state of our body. Paying attention to the ways we *learn* to cook – making bread, for example – we realize that the picture of the human being as a mind with a bodily appendage is a crude cartoon. It simply makes no sense to say that someone theoretically 'knows' how to bake bread, but cannot do it – that they have the understanding of leavening, gluten, time and temperature, kneading and folding down, but can't make their hands perform the related operations. Having a conceptual understanding of yeast and gluten is not what knowing how to make bread is, any more than understanding the theory of internal combustion means being able to repair a carburettor. Likewise, someone whose hands are capable of kneading does not thereby 'know' how to make bread; knowing how to make bread requires one to understand – in a complex, whole-body way – what is happening during that kneading process.

Many thoughtful practices are central to our lives. We believe there is something about food-making that gives its membership in that category a particular savour. Food-making produces things that, when consumed, become us, materially, physically, literally, on a cellular level. When we make food – whether that means tilling the soil to grow a patch of corn, or stirring water into a boxed cornbread mix and smoothing the batter into a pan – we are creating something external that will become internal. That makes food-making different in kind from making a musical instrument, a piece of furniture, a sweater, a computer, or virtually any other thing that we make. Many objects that we create become *extensions* of our person – our clothing, our pens, our phones, the tools of our trade – but they remain (or most do) outside us.[17]

In the spirit of the contemporary feminist philosopher of science and technology Donna Haraway, we acknowledge that humans *are* cyborgs; we are elaborate composites of fleshy stuff and manufactured implants, additions, enhancements. (The parents of one of us – with two pacemakers and three hearing aids between them – used to say that they 'ran on batteries'. They weren't kidding: without those batteries, not only would they have been inconvenienced, they would have died.) So we do not mean to make food magical and 'uniquely unique'. Nevertheless, it remains true that, since our earliest ancestors came into existence, we humans have been taking the edible 'not me' and making it 'me'. There is an elemental quality to eating things that makes it extremely different from having a smartphone (which can become an extension of one's hand almost literally, and can become one's 'external memory', but can be placed on the bureau at night). It is also quite different from having a pacemaker, despite the fact that the pacemaker is internal. A pacemaker can still be extracted from one's body; the cherries you ate last night cannot. The fact that the 'not me' is completely absorbed into the 'me' makes food-making activities potent for understanding the nature of human inquiry.

As a final way to explain why human–food interactions make excellent incubators in which to reflect on the nature of inquiry and knowing, we would note just a few of the ways in which philosophers have linked knowing with eating (as distinct from food-making). Plato suggests that humans' digestive tracts are well suited to our identities as creatures of intelligence. In his *Timaeus*, he suggests that the prodigious length of our intestinal tract enables us to think for long periods of time, uninterrupted by the 'beast' chained in our stomachs.[18] (Such a view of course creates some other problems for us, insofar as it treats parts of ourselves as somehow external to ourselves. Is hunger really best understood as a beast in our belly? Nevertheless, the acknowledgement is a starting point.)

More interesting still are those philosophers who regard eating as a metaphor or model for knowing – eating *as* knowing. Both Plato and John Dewey use eating in these ways. In the *Theaetetus*, Plato compares and contrasts the dangers of inquiry to the dangers of eating. Both eating and inquiry involve taking something into and making it a part of oneself; in the case of eating you can at least take food home in a vessel and inspect it *before* ingesting it, whereas knowledge goes right into us, with no time for inspection. Note that part of the reason Plato's metaphor is so powerful is that it plays on our understanding that food does enter into us and become us. Like knowledge, it can help or harm us. Both involve risks. Knowledge can disrupt our comfortable lives; foods can sicken us. The alternatives, though, are not especially attractive: ignorance and death. (Not attractive either, when we think about it, is a completely risk-free life. Achievement and the satisfaction it brings disappear when the possibility of failure is never real.)

In *Experience and Nature*, Dewey offers an analogy with eating that suggests something quite useful for our project. He takes up a question that really bothers mind-centred philosophers: how can we know anything about the external world? Dewey offers a simple rejoinder. He suggests that the problem of how a mind can know something external to itself 'is like the problem of how an animal eats things external to itself'.[19] Indeed, he points out, it is only things external to ourselves that we reach out to and *can* eat – and the same is true of learning, or coming to know. Dewey well realized that philosophy as it has come to be understood was no place for someone interested in any sort of 'hand work'. Let's face it: philosophy hasn't been a particularly safe place even to admit that you are bodily (that you 'have a body', as philosophers like to put it). Philosophy, since the time it emerged and coalesced in ancient Greece as an activity with a name, has been aimed primarily at getting us as far away as possible from the kinds of activities that are lumped under names such as 'practical', 'craft' or 'everyday' – activities that 'keep body and soul together', as we often say. Food-making falls entirely within this category. Philosophy, as some of its major fans and practitioners have envisioned it, is strictly 'head work' – reflection, abstraction, theorization. Dewey is one of the few philosophers who worked to reconstruct such traditional divisions. As a result he proves particularly useful for discussions of the significance of food-making for understanding the nature of inquiry.

In *The Quest for Certainty* (1929), Dewey points out that humans, throughout their history, have been trying to 'escape from peril' – that is, escape from the peril that is human existence, with all its tenuousness, uncertainty, instability, chaos and downright disastrousness. Another way to phrase this, as suggested in Chapter One, is as an 'escape from responsibility', a desire to skirt the need to make decisions in situations characterized by uncertainty. As a result of the desire to escape from peril, one move was to turn oneself away from matters of this (unreliable) world and towards the (permanent, unchanging, reliable) affairs of another – be it the realm of God or the realm of Ideas. This realm (utterly separate from the everyday world in which things rot or break) is knowable because it is unchanging. Such security makes it attractive as a refuge from peril. As a result, Dewey says, it came to be praised as the only truly knowable realm.

Dewey was onto something when he identified one prime reason for the elevation of theory above practice: practical activities are hard, dirty, often dangerous, repetitious and impermanent. In contrast to this, the life of the mind is identified with leisure. This division has been spelled out in social hierarchies that assign manual labour to slaves, serfs, wives and other 'menials', while mind work has been reserved for those members of a society who hold power and authority. A second reason is related to the first one: practical activities (Dewey actually just refers to these things as 'work' at this point) are bodily activities directed at 'material things' – lumps of coal, bolts of cloth, bags of grain – while intellectual activity is conceived of as purely mental work directed at ideas, which are immaterial: 'The disrepute which has attended the thought of material things in comparison with immaterial thought has been transferred to everything associated with practice.'[20] In other words, the theory/practice hierarchy is directly implicated in the mind–body dualism.

Dewey notes that these 'reasons' really just push the matter back a notch. *Why* is the body denigrated? *Why* are practices automatically assumed to be separate from thought? Here Dewey is getting at the heartbeat of philosophy. He does not simply answer questions that have been handed down by the tradition; he wonders about the general orientation that led to the very ways in which those questions were formulated. Why, he asks, 'this invidious discrimination', this 'sharp division between theory and practice' and, crucially for us, how has the separation of intellect from action affected the theory of knowledge?[21] What if the grasp of things which promulgated the divorce were reconsidered? What if knowing and doing were brought (back?) into intrinsic connection with one another? What revisions of the traditional theory of mind, thought and knowing would be required, and what changes in the idea of the office of philosophy would be demanded?

Such questions form the backbone of Dewey's *The Quest for Certainty*; we have followed him some distance, mapping our own course by focusing on the particular ways in which the division of theory and practice has affected the practices we use to provide ourselves with food (growing, processing, preparing and cleaning up after it). We've also followed him in his efforts to heal the rift, showing why and how food-making might be a particularly valuable mode of activity through which to explore and develop our notion of 'thoughtful practice'.

This sketch of an answer to the question 'why food and epistemology?' actually serves another purpose as well. It suggests why our relationships with food have proven to be the sites of such urgent and compelling messes. Recall that philosophy is like plumbing in its ubiquity and all-inclusiveness. One way to describe the ubiquity of philosophy is to observe that every domain of human inquiry has its associated philosophical questions or problems. Food-making and eating are themselves activities that are not only vitally important in some rather brute biological ways; they are also embedded into our religious practices, our cultural and ethnic identities, our social pastimes and virtually all other human institutions and endeavours. They are present in deep, non-trivial ways. Not surprisingly, these different 'uses' of food-making and eating regularly come into contact – and conflict – with each other. As food and cooking have risen in prominence in the public eye in the developed world, perhaps so too have the conflicts risen in intensity and number, along with the perceived need to resolve them satisfactorily.

Current discussions about the concept of sustainability present an interesting case in point. Recall the grocery shopping expedition with which this chapter began. Add 'sustainably grown' to the laundry list of conditions those shoppers may wish to meet, as they spend their limited budget. What, exactly, do we mean by 'sustainably grown?' It turns out that the answer is both 'it depends' and 'it's complicated'. We may point first to environmental considerations and then to economic ones, perhaps adding cultural, ethnic and social concerns a bit later. (What might it mean to say that a food is 'culturally sustainable?' Among other things, that it includes enabling the continued flourishing of cultural traditions, identity and meaning.)

At first reflection, we like to imagine that, if someone says 'how are we to eat?' we can reply 'sustainably'. The assumption is that, with some effort, we can eat food that is sustainable in all these various senses. But, as anyone following the literature, or even simply reading the newspaper, knows, that isn't possible – not even if one expends a lot of effort trying to. What constitutes sustainability in one arena might, and often does, conflict with requirements in another. And quite often, even a single arena such as environmental sustainability involves so many layers and such a complex weave of issues and concerns that they simply cannot all be met simultaneously in some grand moment of 'sustaining'. It's always messy, much as we long for a kind of unified field theory of sustainability. Even the meaning of the term itself is a moving goal.

How do we deal with this mess? Not, we submit, by examining it as would an outside, detached spectator. Such a standpoint leads readily to the either/or of 'here is the one definitive answer' or 'there are no real answers'. Indeed, it is partly because we have inherited those notions that we are mired in particular messes. We would not be disputing the meaning of sustainability as we are today did we not, deep in the recesses of our thinking, still harbour a secret Cartesian belief that there *is* an essence to this concept and all we have to do is *find* it in order for everything to fall into place. Often the realization that no such single answer is available leads thinkers to slide into scepticism.

The approach consistent with our analysis – 'thoughtful practice' associated with 'responsibility as objectivity' – offers a more concrete, ameliorative take on the situation. When we think of ourselves as (i) hungry and (ii) as taster/testers, we encourage ourselves to keep working at better and better resolutions of our difficulties. We are relieved of the false dilemma fostered by the older spectator approach, with its either/or constructions: either I have a perfect vision of things or such a vision is an illusion.

Food-making and eating matter to humans at both the most basic and also the most ephemeral levels. Because our relationships to food are so multifaceted, they risk messiness, and thus available for some philosophical plumbing. This chapter has attempted some of this work by focusing on a set of dichotomies and hierarchies that have formed the core of much of Western philosophy since Plato. These have morphed and changed in significant ways during those centuries; our brief account can do little more than sketch some of its main manifestations. But some things about those dichotomies and hierarchies continue to endure as commonsense beliefs today. As such, they continue to affect the ways we think and behave. Our alternative has, as its main function, precisely to alter these ways of thinking and behaving.

IV

Being Hungry,
Hungry Being

The Soul is Hungry

Sitting on top of a column, St Simeon Stylites ('Simeon of the column', *c.* 388–459) kept food to a bare minimum. His concern: the soul. For over 39 years he followed a dramatic strategy, setting himself up on increasingly tall pillars. For him, caring for the soul required extraordinary, leave-the-world-behind actions. The body Simeon regarded as a nuisance, with hunger and thirst chief among its annoying demands. A dramatic counteroffensive was needed, thus the columnar isolation.

Old St Simeon may seem quaint to us, steeped as we are in a world of bodily pleasures. Still, his way of thinking – considering the body as an obstacle to the spirit – represents a continuing strand in Western thought. Even today's hedonists have simply reversed St Simeon's valorization. They have not abandoned the body versus spirit attitude. This enduring *versus* strand is one important offspring of the great generative idea of modernity we have been challenging in this book: the separation of soul and body.

That dichotomization manifests itself in various diets, which come and go in popularity. Dietary care for the body often translates into one particular form of the opposition 'nature versus culture'. For example, fans of the 'Evo' (evolution) diet assert, as their first rule, 'you should listen to your body and not your culture.'[1] The movement even has a catchy slogan, 'Eat like the apes for optimum health.'² 'Culture' has led us astray. It gave us processed foods high in sugar, fat, refined carbohydrates and sodium. The only way to return our bodies to health, according to the Evo diet, is to adopt a diet that takes us back to our evolutionary roots, one that is mostly raw and vegetarian.³ People with pets can bring them on board with a nutritional programme known affectionately as BARF, 'biologically appropriate raw food'.⁴

Another approach that aims to eliminate culture's unhealthy influence on our diets goes by various labels: instinctotherapy, instinctive nutrition and (for those who like Greek roots) anopsology (meaning 'not-prepared-dish'). 'Instinct' is the key word. Adherents of this movement believe that we instinctively know what is best for us, especially as regards foods. The primatologist Richard Wrangham describes a lunch with followers of the diet:

> They sniffed at several fruits, one at a time, to allow their bodies to decide what would suit them best ('by instinct', they said). One chose apples; another chose a pineapple. Each ate only his or her first choice. The third decided on a protein-rich food. He had brought frozen buffalo steaks and pieces of buffalo femur. Today was a marrow day. The femur chunks were the size of golf balls. Inside each was a cold pink mush that looked like strawberry ice cream. He cleaned out several pieces of bone with a teaspoon.⁵

If only we had not turned away from nature and started cooking our food, then our instincts would work as they had been intended. Since, however, we have elected to remove ourselves from that which is natural, we must work – hard – to recapture our bodies' instinctual capacities to guide our eating choices.

Simeon intellectually separated soul from body. Our contemporaries separate nature from culture. They seek to ward off the corruptions of culture, understood as particularly connected to mental activity. In both cases, it is assumed that some original, pure, more refined state has been corrupted by later accretions.

This 'initial purity, subsequent corruption' pattern plays itself out in our contemporary food messes. Should we go with the 'Evo' diet, or its cousin the 'Paleo' diet? (The latter urges that it is the diet of humans, not that of their simian ancestors, that should be the standard. Humans, this diet holds, 'naturally' eat meat.) Or perhaps we should instead *embrace* culture: cook our food, flavour it with culturally authentic seasonings, refine, shine and polish its surfaces, package it in clever and elaborate ways and take delivery of it daily, via a service that will scientifically design a diet specifically for our metabolism, lifestyle and culinary preferences. We humans, after all, are quite unlike those poor koala bears genetically designed to eat only the leaves of eucalyptus trees. We can freely choose our diets. Indeed, freedom has enabled cultures to develop all manner of unique cuisines. Since such cuisines can take us very far from nature, the nature/culture question has been a constant presence in that reflection on life known as philosophy. The history of that reflection also teaches us how the 'initial purity, subsequent corruption' pattern has not always been the dominant mode of approaching the question of the natural and the cultural.

Had he known Aristotle, St Simeon might have followed a different tack. For Aristotle, soul and nutrition go hand in hand. Why? Because the soul does not stand in opposition to the body. Aristotle considered the need for nourishment as the mark of an 'ensouled' being. Ensoulment was synonymous with a particular kind of functioning. The soul is to the body, he said famously, as seeing is to the eye.[6] The Latin equivalent for soul – *anima*, from which comes the word 'animate' – brings the soul–nutrition connection into even clearer focus. There are many sorts of animate creatures, all of which share the need to feed. Strange as it may sound today, to be ensouled, to be animate – whether plant, animal or human – is to be in need of nourishment.

It sounds odd to us because of our philosophical heritage. Today's common sense, we could say, is yesterday's philosophy, and yesterday's philosophy was not that of Aristotle but that of the post-Renaissance world. By the sixteenth century, philosophers had rejected Aristotle as outdated, adopting instead the generative idea that neatly compartmentalized body and soul. *Versus* became a generalized background assumption. This, in turn, resulted in a way of thinking which eventually associated 'soul' with only one type of animate being: humans.

Soul as a component of human life soon mutated into 'mind', thanks in no small part to René Descartes. As we saw in Chapter Two, it was Descartes who gave the post-seventeenth-century ('modern') generative idea its real boost. In several influential works, he crystallized the *versus* attitude, the sequestering of mind from body and, thus, 'man' from the rest of the natural world. Descartes did not invent this move. Many strands in medieval religious philosophy had prepared the way for it; the Cartesian formulations simply helped cement the transformation. One by-product of this was that those older continuities between vegetative, animal and human souls – the three Aristotelian varieties of ensoulment – faded from use. 'Soul' became an exclusive property of humans, and thus needed a new name to distinguish it from that older tradition. 'Mind', at once both more secular and more readily isolable from the concrete living organism, did the trick.

As we have seen, the 'dichotomize everything' approach turned adjectives and adverbs into nouns; intelligent and physiological dimensions came to be reified as 'mind' and 'body'. Since 'body' was shared with other creatures while 'mind' was not, the latter came to be understood as the unique 'essence' of humanity. Whatever was not mind could only be considered incidental to the genuinely human dimension. 'Man' became what the philosophers called him: the 'rational animal', where 'rational' meant everything and 'animal' signified little more than a hairy container.

'Mind', separate from 'body', now carried all the weight of one's real self. In fact, the very word 'self' as a noun had not been prominent until the philosopher John Locke (1632–1704) felt the need to make a substantive from a modifier.[7] Once the modifier-to-noun shift had been made, a particular kind of issue could be raised: what if, Locke asked, the mind of a prince moved into the body of a cobbler? Would the personhood of the prince remain unchanged? Yes, was Locke's answer. This is because the real self is a kind of inner, immaterial unit; our bodily casing represents little more than a sort of outer shell. Like clothing, it can be changed without affecting our identity. The prince might wonder why he suddenly has a hankering for cheap beer rather than fine wine or why stewed rabbit suddenly tastes better than spit-roasted hog, but these appetites are incidental matters, unconnected to his soul/mind/self, which is no longer hungry. The prince remains a prince regardless of the new bodily structure he occupies.

Though the moderns would no doubt have disdained the extreme behaviour of St Simeon, they nevertheless inadvertently followed his example in one important way: the flesh-and-blood human being, the hungry creature, could now be disregarded, even more completely than St Simeon could have accomplished with his pillar-sitting. As we have seen already, philosophers simply made the body inessential. Descartes called humans 'thinking things'; Kant, 'rational agents'. The fact of being hungry cannot be gainsaid, but it can, for all *philosophical* intents and purposes, remain unheeded. Yesterday's philosophy is indeed today's common sense; our twenty-first-century talk is still filled with language that understands the mind as separate, disembodied and decidedly un-hungry. One task of a stomach-inclusive philosophy like ours is to change that language, by shifting the general orientation.

Metaphysics

The sharp separation of things into a class that possesses mind and one that does not exemplifies a general description of reality that goes by the formidable philosophical name 'metaphysics'. The word has acquired a muddled set of meanings because it was, originally, a misnomer. Aristotle had written some texts which he referred to as 'basic' or 'fundamental' philosophy. An editor, placing these works after the ones dealing with nature ('physics' in Greek), titled them 'Metaphysics' – that is, 'those texts that come after the physics'. Since then, 'metaphysics' has become linked with views that seek to leave behind the world of ordinary experience.

Our alternative, that of a palpable, stomach-centred take on things, sets out to plot a different course. We begin by reconnecting ourselves with that cluster of beings to which we have historically belonged: the ensouled or animate sorts of beings. Within that group, we gladly admit what is obvious: we all require nutrition. Indeed, this important fact will now play a role in philosophy similar to the role it plays in ordinary life – that is to say, a fundamental one. Any general perspective on the way things are – any 'metaphysics' – will be sadly misguided if it leaves out the need for nourishment and all that comes with such a need.

To get a sense of the differences our revised idea will make, we begin with plants, the beings Aristotle described as possessing 'vegetative souls'. A plant's life, as described in the words of W. H. Auden, 'is one continuous solitary meal'.[8] Plants are, in a sense, always 'eating'. But Auden was only partly correct. While plants are the least mobile of living things, they are anything but 'solitary'. Indeed, their interdependency is part of what makes them an ideal starting point for our metaphysics.

For a less poetic but more scientifically reliable insight into this interconnectedness, we turn to the French botanist who founded the European Institute for Ecology. Jean-Marie Pelt has spent his career bringing to light the manifold interdependencies that mark the world of living things, particularly trees, shrubs and flowers. When it comes to plant nutrition, he identifies three historical stages. In the 1950s, the model was simple; Auden's 'solitary meal' seemed an accurate description. Trees, using photosynthesis at one end and roots drawing in nutrients at the other, were understood to feed in a mostly autonomous fashion. Solitary feeding seemed to rule. A tree may have been part of a cluster in a dense forest but, nutritionally speaking, it was on its own.

A couple of decades later, things started to get more complicated. Further research revealed that the roots of trees were covered with bacteria. Not only that, but pesky local fungi managed to extend their filaments and wrap them around the roots. In the old way of thinking, one's first reaction might be: 'Oh no, would that the tree could get hold of some good antibiotics and fungicides. Would that its solitary meal were not disturbed by these interlopers who are no doubt stealing its nutrients.' Such a judgement would be both hasty and faulty. The fungi and bacteria, although foreign agents, turned out to be helpful. Without the fungi and the bacteria, the tree would go hungry. Trees' meals may be continuous, but they are far from solitary. They are raucous banquets featuring multiple life forms from different kingdoms.

By the turn of the twenty-first century, a third, even more complicated phase emerged. Researchers came to realize that 'in the soil, there existed a "web" distributing nutrition just as the Internet distributes information.'[9] One fascinating beneficiary of this nutritional network is an odd flower, the Indian pipe or ghost plant (*Monotropa uniflora*). This plant looks more like a mushroom than a flower, having no green coloration. It lives in dark places. It does not depend on photosynthesis. On the 'solitary meal' view of things, it's a bit of a loser. It cannot feed itself – so really a big-time loser. How, then, does it survive? It 'borrows' nutrients.

This particular flower satisfies its nutritional needs by drawing from the roots of pine trees. In one sense this procedure might not seem so unusual. After all, parasitic plants, like the well-known mistletoe, regularly engage in such borrowing. Typically, though, such species attach themselves directly to their hosts. Not so the Indian pipe. Its nutrition comes via the assistance of an interlinked underground grid in which the pathways for channelling nutrients are mushrooms. These mycorrhizal fungi exist in a symbiotic relationship with roots. When it comes to *M. uniflora*, the fungi act as a conduit, moving the energy that comes from a tree's photosynthetic capacities, through the roots, via the fungus to the Indian pipe.[10]

Pelt's three stages help us to locate a historical trajectory for our new ground map of metaphysics. Taking its cue from plant nutrition, this revised map shifts the emphasis from solitariness and self-sufficiency to interdependence. Hunger has always been problematic for those who would privilege autonomy and self-sufficiency, for those who separate the mind from the body. After all, hunger specifies a need for something outside oneself, a need that must be satisfied if the mind is going to carry out 'its' work. But, thinking old-style, 'Being', in the fullest and best sense of that concept, would surely never be hungry. Hunger, considered from the vantage point of self-sufficiency, denotes deficiency, incompleteness, dependency. By contrast, a stomach-sensitive metaphysics understands hunger, and more generally 'neediness', as *defining* existence, not something to be ashamed of. On this model, 'Being' – even model, ideal being – is hungry. Always hungry. For *something*.

Hungry Being

Discussions of metaphysics can quickly become both overly technical and hopelessly arcane. Hoping to avoid both problems, we begin with a straightforward distinction: between the 'metaphysics of self-sufficiency' and the 'metaphysics of interdependence'. Within a metaphysics of self-sufficiency, *non*-dependence and *non*-neediness are (i) identified as basic and (ii), valorized. They serve as markers of ideal, paradigmatic existence. Such a metaphysical starting point would lead inquirers to begin by assuming that our world is populated by separate, individual, independent entities; individual bits of buckshot littered about the sphere. Such inquirers would also, naturally, aspire to live lives that are maximally autonomous and self-sufficient.

The metaphysics of interdependence establishes a different take on things. It accepts linkages, connections, interrelationships and the neediness that accompanies these as not only real, but fundamental. Autonomous, self-sufficient units are recognized as fictions – useful fictions sometimes, perhaps, but not beings who could really survive in such a state. They are products of a conceptual abstraction that artificially isolates them from the webs within which they exist. Auden's poetic reference to the 'solitary' plant meal, while lovely and lyrical, simply fails to appreciate the literal web of relations that enables the plant to be nourished.

An important ethical corollary emerges from these contrasting metaphysical positions and brings our discussion full circle back to that of Chapter One. Hospitality, built upon the notion of mutual dependence and neediness, finds no prominent place in a metaphysics of self-sufficiency. Why is this? Dependence and neediness automatically become pejorative. Self-reliance and autonomy, attitudes not exactly conducive to hospitality, become guiding values. Fullness of being – the ideal to strive for – is no longer that of fashioning an open, welcoming home, as it was for Baucis and Philemon. Hunger is no longer the starting point from which hospitality becomes a main obligation. In a metaphysics of self-sufficiency, it would be *better* (an important ethical term) if hunger did not force us into dependent relationships. The sought-after state, the state of most complete realization of one's being, is self-containment; acting as one's own emergency kit.

By contrast, for the metaphysics of hungry being, dependencies are basal and irreducible. Even more strongly put, self-containment is now recognized as incompatible with a full, flourishing life. It is only by focusing exclusively on our mental life and ignoring our gastral one that we can even begin to think of ourselves as separate, bounded, 'auto-sufficient' units. St Simeon Stylites may have envisioned himself as something like Auden's plant, eating a 'solitary meal', but of course this was far from the case. Though he ate and drank little, he still depended upon (i) people and (ii) nature's bounty for the food and drink that made its way to him atop his column. Both of these factors tend to be rendered invisible in those accounts of the behaviour of saints written from the point of view of a metaphysics of self-sufficiency.

Un-blinkered once we move beyond the metaphysics of self-sufficiency, we come to realize that it is not only other people and nature's bounty on which we humans rely. Like the Indian pipe, we too depend upon other organisms to do our digesting for us. In our case, the help comes in the form of a vast colony of bacteria, whose members outnumber the cells in our own bodies. As little food as he may have eaten, St Simeon still needed his companion bacteria to help him digest. Our appetites, even voracious ones, would be of little survival value were it not for those microbial eaters in our guts. So important are these microbes that scientists believe we should not refer to ourselves as single discrete units. A more accurate label for the conglomeration that is the human would be 'super-organism',[11] yet another indication that the metaphysics of self-sufficiency was based on a simplified, abstract understanding of ourselves and our situation in the world. That abstract understanding led to certain formulations becoming common and almost second nature. The move to a metaphysics of interdependence brings these into question. We will highlight three of them that touch our ordinary ways of living: the culture–nature relation, freedom and authenticity.

Culture and Nature

Going back to the Greeks, we already find competing positions regarding the proper way to understand culture and nature. The contrast can be summarized as 'Homer versus Diogenes'. Homer celebrates hospitality, communal meals and the cultural practices that make them central. Diogenes of Sinope (412?–323 BCE) flees the artificiality of 'culture', preferring simple, raw food eaten alone. This means that the early Homeric world, very long ago, was actually closer to our 'new' metaphysics than was the world of Diogenes, centuries later. Actually, some 500 years after Homer, the Hellenistic era marked the beginning of a concerted and lengthy move in the direction of self-sufficiency metaphysics, a direction well exemplified by Diogenes and the school to which he belonged, the Cynics.

Fundamental to the way the Cynics established their bearings was a simple aspiration: they sought to avoid the false pretentions of 'culture' and live according to 'nature'. Also, appropriately enough, they did not think of humans as little gods who could create norms out of nothing. One way or another, humans must take guidance from somewhere. They chose nature. The Cynics practised living according to what they believed was nature's unadulterated model.

What philosophers realize is that words like 'nature' do not come with a ready-made, limited definition. They have a history, and that history reveals varieties of meaning. One important task of philosophy is to investigate those meanings, paying particular attention to what they entail, asking about what follows when a particular meaning comes to hold sway across an entire culture. For Diogenes, the opposition of nature to culture made plenty of sense because it was *already* embedded in a world dominated by the lure of self-sufficiency. Put another way, this model of nature entails a denigration of all dependencies – including, of course, those represented by the stomach.

Terms such as 'nature' have meanings only within a wider setting of metaphysical assumptions. If 'to be' is understood in its fullest sense to entail self-sufficiency, then the more 'natural' a person is, the more self-reliant that person is. Living according to nature will then involve, as it did for Diogenes, an attempt to minimize dependencies of all sorts. Indeed, Diogenes satisfied himself with a meagre diet made up mostly of what he could beg from others. He went around with only a ladle for scooping up water. When he saw a child achieve the same end by simply using his hands, he tossed the ladle away.

The ancient chroniclers are full of entertaining anecdotes about Diogenes. One of his pupils was named Crates. On his wedding night, Crates and his bride consummated their marriage in public. (After all, Cynics were committed to the goodness and innocence of living according to nature. What could be more natural than copulation?) This public lovemaking went one better than even Diogenes', whose own version was single-handed. Having been chastised for masturbating in public, he replied with a self-sufficiency-tinged food metaphor: 'I only wish I could relieve hunger by rubbing my stomach.'[12]

The important lesson for us is that a particular exhortation such as 'live according to nature' does not have a fixed, cross-temporal, cross-cultural meaning independent of metaphysics. A background network of assumptions gives particular content to certain concepts. Philosophers aim to unearth those assumptions, as well as provide richer, more fruitful ones. A food-friendly philosophy will, of necessity, provide alternative pathways of its own.

To begin with, it will appreciate the integration between culture and nature, a link powerfully exemplified by agriculture. In agriculture, continuity and interplay, not separation and isolation, predominate. None of the key features – soil, sun, rain, seeds, predators, diseases – is invented by 'culture'. Each belongs to the natural realm. But neither do these 'natural' entities give rise by themselves to the kinds of products that make their way to our tables; even 'wild' mushrooms have sprung up in soil that has been shaped by human (cultural) activity. Cultures emerge within settings of cultivation – the deliberate propagation and nurturing of particular food plants. Notably, and as another sign of continuity, we also use the word 'cultivation' to describe the effort to guide children to proper maturity.

In his great food-filled novel *The History of Tom Jones, A Foundling* (1749), the English author Henry Fielding wrote of 'breeding' in a way that also stressed the relationship of interweaving that obtains between nature and culture. In contemporary speech, the verb 'to breed' tends to have primarily physiological connotations, and rather crass ones at that; young heterosexual couples with many children might be referred to pejoratively as 'breeders', for instance. For Fielding, the term still also indicated the cultural practices associated with 'bringing up' a child. In the novel, a squire (with the significant name, Allworthy) has adopted a foundling. He resolves 'to breed him up as his own',[13] an expression that indicates the (cultural) cultivating of the possibilities inherent in 'raw material'. In the case of a foundling, that raw material is of uncertain, perhaps dubious, provenance, making the 'breeding' all the more important.

In more recent years, some scholars have been paying attention to a link between human cultures and the specific activities of 'culturing' food – that is, fermenting it. The fermentation expert Sandor Katz fondly observes that without cultured foods, there is no culture; the wines and cheeses of France and Italy, the kimchi of Korea and the garri of West Africa are fermented foodstuffs whose identity is intimately tied to the identity of those regions' civilizations. That common word is revelatory. Several of the various meanings of 'culture', including those having to do with the world of biology and others with the 'life of the mind', overlap and interpenetrate.

As these examples indicate, our language ('culturing', 'breeding') retains hints of an orientation that once recognized a continuity and interplay between natural dispositions and their cultivation. Once again, the transformation of modifiers such as 'natural' and 'cultural' into nouns makes abstract – rather than concrete – thinking more amenable. The sharp separation between 'nature' and 'culture' is neat and tidy; it appeals to the kind of rational grids favoured by supporters of self-sufficiency metaphysics. When concrete circumstances challenge such a metaphysics, it creates the opportunity for an alternative. Within the metaphysics of interdependence, cultural developments can be understood not in sharp opposition to nature, but as the manifestation of possibilities latent within the natural realm itself. History and anthropology reveal how wide is the range of such possibility.

Freedom

Besides setting up a sharp division between nature and culture, the metaphysics of self-sufficiency affects other ordinary ways of articulating our situation. One wide-ranging impact involves the ideal of freedom. Here too, the general context is crucial. In settings that prize anti-dependence and anti-neediness, 'freedom' will be understood as that which is disengaged as much as possible from external influences. Often it will be associated with something called 'free will'. 'Free will' is, in turn, envisioned as a faculty outside the flow of natural processes. So dominant has this approach become that even today the issue of freedom is most often phrased in terms of 'free will'. People will not ask, 'do you believe humans have freedom?' Rather they will ask 'do you believe in free will?' The two questions, though, have not always been synonymous.

For an early philosopher such as Socrates, freedom meant the ability to chart one's course and live it out in practice. In particular, it meant avoiding both arbitrariness and capriciousness. The kind of expression contemporary Americans often use, namely, 'this is a free country and I'll eat whatever I please, whenever I please', would have seemed badly misguided to Socrates. Such a person – snacking in the car, eating ice cream at all hours of the night, breaking into the children's Halloween candy – would be the very picture of an enslaved soul, one not at all in control of itself. Freedom was synonymous neither with arbitrariness nor with unfettered indulgence. Full, active freedom meant understanding what was good for a human being, charting a course that would bring about such goods, and then actually being able to live out that course of action.

Humans, for Socrates, were free and in control of their lives when they lived according to what they understood as the proper arrangement of their desires. Such a person might say, 'I have liberated myself from the false desires and temptations of eating ice cream three times a day.' Truly free persons would live in ways that corresponded with the insight of the wisest members of the community – ways that might seem terribly constrained to someone raised on the 'free country' way of thinking.

The strange ability to pick out options and act on them, regardless of context, physiological conditions or merit – the ability we label 'free will' – would have been worse than worthless to Socrates; it would have been downright dangerous. Far from ignoring context, he understood living freely as requiring that one pay careful attention to the conditions that constrain a human life, and chart an intelligent course through them. Admitting temporal, contextual and physiological constraints only made sense. What counted as evidence of freedom were concrete results: people in charge of their lives –lives guided by intelligence and experience.

The other notion of freedom, the form associated with the metaphysics of self-sufficiency, is well represented by a fascinating figure whose work is filled with illustrations involving food: the French-Swiss philosopher Jean-Jacques Rousseau (1712–1778). Rousseau was self-taught, a musician, an educational reformer and a champion of democracy. He also wrote an early 'let-it-all-hang-out' autobiography, the *Confessions*. He is perhaps infamous for having fathered, and immediately placed into orphanages, five children. Like Descartes, Rousseau had a knack for crystallizing themes that were present yet diffuse in the culture of the time. In that regard, the eighteenth-century thinker articulated patterns that seeped into the intellectual climate at large, leaving a deposit still widely felt today. The metaphysics of self-sufficiency imbued all of Rousseau's work in the form of certain assumptions which shaped the very way in which he framed questions.

We get a clear sense of how Rousseau understood freedom when we look at how he explored the mess he believed afflicted eighteenth-century Europeans: 'Man is born free, and everywhere he is in chains.'14 Rousseau certainly had a skill for turning an attention-grabbing phrase. Yet 'attention-grabbing' does not necessarily mean 'defensible'. Although he voiced it as a straightforward historical claim, we can recognize Rousseau's assertion as tinged with metaphysical assumptions, including that of a sharp separation between culture and nature. By nature, he suggests, we are in possession of genuine liberty. That liberty gets chipped away as we come, more and more, to be domesticated and eventually enslaved by culture.

Rousseau makes this understanding of the human condition explicit in his book *Émile; or, On Education*, a treatise on the proper upbringing of young men: 'Everything is good as it leaves the hands of the Author of things; everything degenerates in the hands of man.'[15] His recognition of the corrupting influence of humans leads him to offer important parenting advice. Because the cultural imposition of habits limits natural freedom, the parent should resist the urge: 'The only habit a child should be allowed is to contract none.'[16] Rousseau specifically targets mealtime habits. When children are raised with regular schedules for eating, their connection with nature is severed. Then, 'desire no longer comes from need but from habit, or, rather, habit adds a new need to that of nature. This is what must be prevented.'[17]

Food practices are significant for Rousseau in other ways as well. Our need for nutrition, as deep a 'natural' need as one could expect, serves as a blueprint for Rousseau's general perspective. If we want to do our children a great favour, we will allow natural tendencies to take their course. Nature knows best. The palate guides what 'suits our stomach'; there is no 'doctor surer for man than his own appetite'.[18]

One hears echoes of Rousseau's thought in those contemporary diets designed to help adults get back in contact with the 'hunger instinct'. The website of one such programme asks, 'If you're not eating to satisfy hunger, then why are you eating?' It goes on to claim: 'Essential to survival, hunger is your cue to take care of your body's natural need for energy and nutrients. Hunger is a *physical* feeling. It's not the same thing as appetite, cravings, or just wanting to eat.'[19] Rousseau's view that culture destroys our natural capacities to eat freely and well finds its contemporary instantiation in the view that 'other triggers, perhaps the time of day, appetizing food, boredom, or stress . . . ' come to be *interpreted* as a 'need for energy and nutrients' – that 'hunger' and 'appetite' are two separate, unrelated things.

Whereas culture is artificial and contrived, nature is plain, direct, unadorned, almost austere. No one, Rousseau asserts, is disgusted by the simple fare of water or bread. The ethical impulse, the 'ought' impulse, emerges consistently from this; 'the most natural tastes ought also to be the simplest.' Translated into advice, this means that adults should aim 'to preserve in the child his primary taste'. After all, 'that is the trace left by nature.' As such, it should be the rule we follow.[20] A simple diet is the best diet. 'Best', we wish to emphasize, means for Rousseau 'most in line with nature'. 'Nature', in turn, means something quite apart from 'culture'. When we give the stomach 'other rules than those of nature' we make a major blunder. Eventually, things get really bad. It is our 'whims' (read: artificial, non-natural appetite, cravings) that guide us rather than our 'stomachs' (read: natural, simple and thus good).[21]

The pattern in Rousseau's handling of food serves as a blueprint for his treatment of freedom. Is freedom a good thing? Naturally. But what exactly is meant by freedom? In his answer to this question, Rousseau definitely sides with Diogenes. Two elements illustrate his particular conception of freedom, a conception that is part of a familiar pattern in Western thought. First, there is his advice against the inculcation of habits. This is of the 'leave me alone, don't tell me what to do' school of freedom. Second is his claim that our original state was mostly idyllic. This claim fits into the 'golden age' scenario (of which the most famous version is the biblical story of the Garden of Eden). The scenario is familiar: (a) there was once an innocent original epoch; (b) some flaw, error, ignorance or other misstep led to a 'fall'; and (c) since that time we have had to figure out how best to recapture the happy initial state.

Within such a story, chains (after the fall) and habits (imposed on nature) intersect. The initial, idyllic state is one of maximal freedom; minimal demands are placed on 'man' (the gender-specific term is intentional). Rousseau's version of this story, a fanciful description of the 'state of nature', is significant for the way it reveals his assumptions. Originally, natural man was a robust sort; if he were not, nature would soon see to his elimination.[22] Hunger, not surprisingly, presents a source of anguish. Robustness and natural skills come to the rescue. Distress is minimized. Need and satisfaction follow each other seamlessly: 'I see him satisfying his hunger under an oak tree, quenching his thirst at the first stream, finding his bed at the foot of the same tree that supplied his meal; and thus all his needs are satisfied.'[23] Man, more flexible than other animals, 'finds his sustenance more easily'.[24]

'Finds his sustenance more easily' by *nature*, Rousseau might as well say. When culture enters the mix, men undergo the fate of domesticated animals: loss of vigour. The 'ways of society' lead man to become 'weak, fearful, and servile; his soft and effeminate lifestyle completes the enervation of both his strength and his courage.'[25] Thankfully, unlike animals, man is still 'a free agent'. Man's free agency raises him above 'physics'. He possesses a will, a faculty unconstrained by the physical, natural, physiological conditions that make up his constitution. Exercising his freedom of will involves man in 'purely spiritual acts', acts outside the scope of the 'laws of mechanics'.[26] In addition, the human possesses the capacity for 'self-perfection'. All of this draws him to strive beyond his natural state and 'out of that original condition in which he would pass tranquil and innocent days'.[27]

As the discussion of freedom develops, Rousseau reveals his commitment to the metaphysics of self-sufficiency. Neediness and dependencies provide man's main foes. Hunger may be unavoidable, but, for Rousseau's idyllic imagination, appetite, in the state of nature, was easily sated; no serious dependence resulted from it.[28] Not only hunger for food, but other natural desires too were satisfied without producing unnatural dependency. What were these other desires? In addition to 'nourishment', they included 'a woman and rest'.[29] Women, like food, were important as transitory sources of satisfaction. Permanent relationships were unknown in nature. Rousseau went on: 'Since nobody had houses or huts or property of any kind, each one bedded down in some random spot and often for only one night.'[30] An appropriate slogan for Rousseau's 'innocent' state could have been 'meet, mate and move on'. Anything else would have smacked of not only neediness but also, horror of horrors, dependence.

Neediness and dependency, for Rousseau, signify not only a lack but, more significantly, an entanglement that marks a clear step towards culture and away from freedom. His view does not consider the possibility that neediness and entanglement might have their positive sides; that, for example, it might be good to have people on whom we can depend, or it might be good to be goaded by a force that counterbalances our tendencies to turn in on ourselves. Socrates and Aristotle had identified needs as key indicators explaining why humans were predisposed to live in communities. For these Greek thinkers, humans inclined *by nature* to actualize possibilities that lead to cultural life.[31] Rousseau specifically rejects such an approach. Nature, he says, cared little 'to bring men together through mutual needs'. He finds it impossible to imagine 'why, in that primitive state, one man would have a greater need for another man than a monkey or a wolf has for another of its respective species'.[32]

It is hard for Rousseau and his descendants to imagine neediness as anything but pejorative. It represents a privation pure and simple. It is also hard for them to avoid an important corollary: dependence is a sign of weakness and decadence. 'Man is weak when he is dependent and he is emancipated from that dependence before he is robust.'[33] A first clue to what causes a shift from robust independence to effeminate dependence comes when we return to the three needs identified by Rousseau: nourishment, a woman and rest. Nourishment and rest pose no real problems. When hungry, we eat. When tired, we sleep. Neither food nor sleep places demands on us, asks us to take out the garbage, help get supper ready or change a diaper. But alas, for Rousseau the third need, 'a woman', brings just these kinds of freedom-restricting demands.

True to his Diogenes lineage, the sharp nature/culture divide colours Rousseau's thinking. We must distinguish, he asserts, the physical from the moral aspects of love. The physical just drives us to unite with another. The moral aspect of love, on the other hand, 'is an artificial sentiment born of social custom, and extolled by women with so much skill and care in order to establish their hegemony and make dominant the sex that ought to obey'.[34] As society, that artificial realm contrived by the female, expands in its reach, so does dependence. As this dependence increases, something else decreases: freedom.

Food, in Rousseau's world view, plays an ever more central role. Family life makes one sedentary. It creates new entanglements as humans need to secure nourishment. The pleasures of conjugal life initially masked those incipient chains. Gradually, though, after the development of private property, things began to move inexorably towards more and more dependencies. The need for food occasioned the development of settled agriculture. This, in turn, called forth the need for technology, specifically metallurgy. 'Iron and wheat', says Rousseau, 'have civilized man and ruined the human race.' Eventually, settled life in communities led to mutual comparisons, false vanities, loss of equality, increased violence, and the chains that necessarily accompany societal life. The end result was catastrophic: the entire human race was subjected 'to labour, servitude and misery'.[35]

From our point of view, what is important is how, for Rousseau, freedom is a one-dimensional possession, present already, by nature, at birth. Given such a starting point, freedom could only be diminished the moment humans engaged in shared, cultural existence. The idea that parents might help children enhance their freedom by actively *cultivating* habits, or that mandatory education might be liberatory, or that conjoint activities might actually enhance one's freedom towards accomplishments, are ideas that cannot be easily accommodated in this model. Nor can the idea that, for creatures like ourselves, some combination of cultural practices, intelligence and discipline are necessary to help us learn which inclinations to pursue and which to avoid. For the descendants of Rousseau, freedom cannot be understood as an achievement – as something rooted in natural dispositions guided by intelligence, habit and other humans. Rather, it is an original possession, one that does not require cultivation. It is either present or absent. Anything else would violate the underlying metaphysical assumption: dependence is a mark of imperfect being. Freedom has to mean 'free will' – that is, complete non-dependence.

Rousseau and Authenticity

Rousseau provides instructive examples not only for freedom but for another contemporary desideratum, authenticity. The sharp nature/culture split once again sets out the context. Within this setting not only does authenticity feature prominently as a guiding ideal, but (our readers are probably getting used to this by now) it acquires a specific content. As heirs to this construal, we confront authenticity everywhere. The language of authenticity has become the lingua franca of ordinary life. Consider, for instance, the veneration with which we are supposed to treat 'authentic' Mexican, Vietnamese or Brazilian cuisine. As a guiding ideal for achieving a fulfilling, significant life, this notion of 'authenticity' owes a lot to the metaphysics of self-sufficiency and the associated focus on the mind at the expense of the stomach.

Rousseau formulates, by way of his metaphysics of self-sufficiency, the central contours of the notion of authenticity that prevails still today. As Charles Guignon notes in his informative little book *On Being Authentic* (2004), Rousseau contributed more 'to the idea of authenticity' than anyone else.[36] He goes on to describe key traits associated with Rousseau-inflected authenticity: a distrust of society; the idea of an inner, true self; turning inward as a way of coming into contact with what is genuine; freedom as the liberation from societal constraints; and a sense that our inner experience is driven to externalize itself.[37] In an editorial aside, Guignon points out how familiar and appealing are these themes, especially in the context of our dissatisfaction with the 'social roles, calcified conventions and frenzied busyness of social existence', which we experience as blocking 'our ability to be all that we can be'.[38]

Besides an intuitive sense of its pervasiveness, it only takes a brief online search to validate Guignon's claim about the appeal of a Rousseau-inspired take on authenticity. A quick search of YouTube yields a video of a talk, 'Authentic Lives' by Michael Tsarion. He mentions Nietzsche and Kierkegaard while explaining the importance of 'transitioning to the authentic life, and the traps that society and the media propagate to keep us dumbed down and unquestioning'.[39] When the video concludes, the viewer is offered a selection of recommended videos, which feature 'authentic watches' and 'authentic Italian pizza sauce recipes'. 'Authenticity' appeals because it helps provide some substantive content for the aspiration towards a good and meaningful life. 'Good' and 'meaningful' now equal 'authentic' – who, after all, wants to live a false life? Who prefers factory-prepared pizza sauce to an authentic one cooked-from-scratch? Who wants a life characterized as phony, sham, artificial or hypocritical?

The shift to a perspective that takes hunger seriously removes our aspiration for authenticity from the content that is provided so long as it orbits around Rousseauian philosophy. When we take hunger not simply as a lack, but as an inclination both for moving outside of ourselves and bringing in what is outside, we no longer treat 'hunger', or 'neediness' more generally, as indicators of weakness and deficiency. If our integral self is hungry, then it is needy in crucial and basic ways. *This* 'true' self requires others. Neediness allows fruitions, culminations and fulfilments. If my 'true self' includes inclinations, talents and aspirations to sing opera, or to become a talented cook or to play soccer, those inclinations have to be developed and cultivated in surroundings that will bring them to the right kind of culmination; true selves need others. Philosophy has been slow to accept this fact of human being, one with which the human sciences have long been comfortable. As the anthropologist Clifford Geertz put it, we humans are 'incomplete or unfinished animals who complete or finish ourselves through culture'.[40] Being stomach-endowed means that our 'true' self cannot simply be an 'inner' self that is connected to the external world only accidentally. Indeed, 'inner' and 'outer' are abstractions, modes of simplifying what is more complex. Who we are, our true self, is not an original, finalized given. It is, rather, a *result* of how we, in Geertz's phrase, 'complete or finish ourselves through culture'.

As we have tried to indicate, the stomach offers itself as an appropriate emblem of this interactive process. The 'authentic' stomach is anything but self-sufficient. Hunger, which drives us out of ourselves and which must incorporate what was originally separate from us, is its 'default' state; indeed, when a stomach is unable to feel or express hunger – understood as the need for completion by something outside itself – something is amiss. It is unwell. Furthermore, despite what Rousseau may claim, we are not inherently disposed towards simple modes of satisfaction. Our original, physiological disposition makes of us omnivores, eager to explore our edible world and inclined to experimentation. Hungry beings are in constant, deep, life-changing interplay with the environments in which we are fully embedded. Recall the bacteria that populate our stomachs; are they 'inner' or 'outer?' Our stomachs' microflora develop in direct response to the kinds of food and water we consume; this susceptibility to influence is not a sign of weakness, but of capacity for survival. A concept of authenticity, if it is to be preserved within a metaphysics of interdependence, must be filtered through the acknowledgement of our hungry being.

As we relinquish the notion of a true, inner, pre-fixed *authentic* self, notice that this shift also challenges the notion that an authentic cuisine or dish has some kind of fixed essence that emerges (solely) from its particular context. Multiple versions of great dishes abound – and all vie for the label 'authentic'. Which of the 'authentic' versions is the 'most authentic'? The notion that there can be an answer to that question ceases to make sense once we cease to understand cuisines and dishes as hermetically sealed packets of cultural identity.

The implication is clear: authenticity – of a dish or a cuisine – is not something given, prior to thought, selection, attention and interest. Rather, it is a product. Cuisines are not static cultural productions any more than cultures are static; they are living, dynamic and responsive to 'internal' and 'external' influences. To privilege a fixed, supposedly initial, version of a dish as the 'true' one is to falsify and do violence to the actual situation. Culinary authenticity comes to be understood not as a fixed set of antecedent properties – a kind of 'checklist' against which a dish must be measured – but as a moving target, acknowledging the fact that dishes are constantly evolving in response to old and new contexts and reinterpreting old features of themselves in light of new influences.

Just as it is with food, so too with people. Remaining true to our nature may indeed be a good thing. But when the stomach-endowed dimension is recognized, the meaning of 'remaining true to our nature' has been altered. 'Nature' becomes a conjunction of actualities and possibilities. The possibilities, in turn, can only be brought to culminations and actualizations in some context by some community. Within such communities, concern about excess – worrying about the faulty, misguided, dangerous trappings of a culture – is fine. This does not, however, mean rejecting culture or thinking of it merely as an outer garment covering an already completed inner self. Harmful, misguided, socially pernicious dimensions of culture do need to be excised. But this can be done by selecting, cultivating, pruning and developing other dimensions. In other words, certain cultural recipes can be favoured, encouraged and developed, while others are similarly discouraged or set aside. Such a flexible sense of authenticity is associated with intelligent direction combined with inherited practices. It replaces, in a stomach-inclusive way of thinking, the sense of authenticity inherited from Rousseau involving the peeling away of layers to arrive at a pure, pre-existent original.

Recipes for Life

Homer's *Odyssey* introduces a variety of peoples. Some are civilized, others not so much. How can we tell? From their food practices. Do they tend fields and grow wheat? Do they make bread? Do they welcome strangers? If the answer to these questions is 'yes', then we are in the presence of civilized individuals. Such persons realize how dependent and interconnected they are. Cultivating wheat and baking bread are not the activities of single, isolated units; these processes require a community that lives out an experience that they share with each other and which is rooted in a heritage from which they have learned.

One of the strangest creatures Odysseus encounters is Polyphemus, the Cyclops. In contrast to bread bakers, the Cyclops is a loner, striving for isolation and self-sufficiency. He thus represents in the Greek tradition not an ideal, but a model of iniquity. Civilized humans, because they live in communities, engage in deliberation. Decisions made by the Cyclops are self-generated. A cultivated people, admitting dependence, occupies itself with trade, but there is no evidence of trading in the world of the Cyclops. Cultured peoples travel. The Cyclops has no ships. Hospitable people welcome their guests by offering them food. The Cyclops eats his guests. Civilization goes hand in hand with cooking and conjoint feasting. The Cyclops does not cook; he eats alone. He is close to being a creature of nature. But how different is the state of nature in Homer from that in Rousseau.

Homer's understanding of the nature–culture continuity was given a handy philosophical formulation by the twentieth-century Spanish-born American philosopher George Santayana

(1863–1952). Though he was explaining the position of Aristotle, his formulation could serve as a slogan for the metaphysics of hungry being: 'everything ideal has a natural basis and everything natural an ideal development.'[41] The process Santayana identifies takes us back, in an important sense, to the question with which our Introduction opened this book: 'how are we to eat?' The multiple implications of that question all involve a basic activity: a back-and-forth movement, a give-and-take exchange between certain aspirations and the circumstances within which those aspirations can be realized.

Natural, meteorological, agricultural, economic, techno-logical and social factors blend together in multiple crisscrossing, zigzagging ways. These interactions make clear that, while it might always be possible to set up an outright opposition between abstract terms such as 'mind' and 'body' or 'nature' and 'culture', it is much harder to set up a parallel opposition between a recipe and its ingredients. This setting is actually closer to Santayana's formulation. A recipe *is* the ingredients (the natural dimension), apportioned and blended (the cultural dimension). Notice that this intertwining of natural and cultural elements can recur at several levels: flour, for instance, may be thought of as the (nat-ural) ingredient in bread, but take it back a stage and flour becomes the intertwined product of wheat (natural) and the industrial milling process (cultural).[42] This feature makes cooking a power-ful instantiation of Santayana's point: the ideal and the natural interpenetrate.

'Nature' by itself offers no standards at all. Or, worse, it can provide justification for anything. Seen from one angle, as Charles Guignon points out, being authentic could mean 'to openly express all the rage, raw sexuality and cruelty within you'.[43] Our 'natural' inclinations are manifold, and they call for cultural recipes that emerge from reflection, experience, counsel and guidance. On the other hand, as Santayana points out, the ideals that guide us do not just pop up out of nowhere. They are not artificial grids imposed, cookie-cutter-like, on amorphous dough. Inclinations, desires and impulses taken willy-nilly may not all be worthy of expression. They do, though, provide the first hints, suggestions and, in general, the raw materials for ideals. As with recipes, it is the back and forth that culminates in the best actual practices.[44]

Although recipes and cooking instructions have existed for a long time, they have been ignored by standard philosophy. They, along with the cooking that brings meals to fruition, need to be rescued from their marginalization by the metaphysics of self-sufficiency. Diogenes and the Cyclops have little to do with cooking. For both, living in accordance with nature means consuming the minimally altered food that nature offers. But in fact this move, rather than being a *return* to some more basic, natural state, is actually an *artificial invention*, and an unusual one at that. Eating large quantities of raw food actually runs counter to humans' physiology; in fact we can best fulfil our nutritional and energy needs by using heat to transform the plants and animals we consume – that is, by cooking them.[45] 'No beast is a cook', James Boswell famously noted.[46] By contrast, humans are, dare we say *by nature*, cooks. Or better stated adjectivally, by *natural* dispositions we are *cultural*. Cooking makes perfect sense for creatures like us. Cooking is not 'unnatural', not a step *away* from nature. It is not, at its core, a simple imposition of artifice.[47]

Instead of some single, already finalized, configuration, some imagined initial state to which we are recalled, the metaphysics of interdependence insists on an irreducible ongoing tension. As is the case with the process that leads from ingredients to finished meal, we are not confronted either with an already existing product, nor do we simply impose an artificial grid. Our inclinations intersect with nature's plants and animals. The starting point is not one or the other in isolation, but both in tension. Inclinations and ingredients together provide the point of departure for the process that will lead to the answer to our question 'how are we to eat? The inclination/ingredient mix calls for cultivation, for some selection and channelling. Not every mode of selection, channelling and cultivation will work well. Human needs are neither neutral nor infinitely malleable. It is a similar case with ingredients: they are neither neutral nor infinitely malleable. Only experimentation, careful observation and shared experiences will generate optimal combinations. But even then, we do not achieve a static, fixed state of 'satisfaction'; hunger always returns. The tension is truly irreducible. The question 'how are we to eat?' is always present.

The circumstances that envelop us do not provide already formulated, universally accessible, finalized directives. Nor, on the other hand, do the circumstances constitute a nihilistic realm, a complete absence of indicators. There are signs; our surroundings offer markers, guidelines, hints – nothing more. There are also cultural traditions that hand down how those markers, guidelines and hints have been read, understood, interpreted and cultivated into valorizations and guidelines. Salt, cinnamon, apples, butter and sugar can be combined in various ways. The one fixed, perfect recipe for blending and cooking them is not just lying out there somewhere. At the same time, a recipe is not a pure invention, a mere construction imposed on a neutral, featureless reality. The ideal and the natural intermingle. Food-making involves the active participation of humans, but always in combination with the features, possibilities and limitations provided by the plants and animals that will become foodstuffs.

When we switch from *self-sufficiency* metaphysics to *needy being* metaphysics, we leave behind the self-enclosed model of human life. On this model, standards must either be 'objective' (self-evidently obvious and clear) or 'subjective' (entirely constructed). Hungry being metaphysics substitutes a response/responsibility model, one in which our task is to engage in 'recipe making' – that is to say, responding to our circumstances as best we can: experimenting with our surroundings, translating traces and clues, materials and methods into workable formulations for optimal forms of life. The 'live according to nature' types were not all wrong. They knew that the 'simply invent' position was untenable. At the same time, the 'invent' position was itself not totally wrong. There is plenty of room for experimentation. The natural calls out for the ideal.

Neat oppositions might suit tidy-minded rationalists. But philosophers, those who seek wisdom, should not be confused with tidy-minded rationalists. We must be careful of philosophical assertions presented as dramatic overstatements, sharply dichotomous alternatives. Such positions typically result from distilling pure ideas from the more amalgamated mixtures present in ordinary life. The word 'distil' is instructive here: in distilling water, one leaves behind all the impurities that cloud ice cubes and clog irons. Having left all of this behind, or, more accurately, having made the active effort to *eliminate* so much, a 'pure' water results. Notably the eliminative effort has also removed everything that gives the water flavour and sparkle. The distilled product is flat, not interesting to drink, unsuitable for cooking and hard on water pipes. Everyday cooking, on the other hand, specializes in creating 'impure' mixtures. It's not that purifying and separating are never useful – try to whip egg whites that have not been separated scrupulously – it's that those pure separations are anything but the norm, anything but the primordial. As it is in cooking, so is it in metaphysics.

Such considerations provide some immediate lessons for reconstructing philosophy. One empirical consideration: do not forget the stomach. Once philosophers forgot, or, we would say, deliberately marginalized the stomach, certain consequences followed. It then made sense to highlight the static, the single, the bounded, the isolated, the self-sufficient. Many a philosopher, and many individuals, have worked and continue to work within this construal. The important reminder we insist upon is this: in order to get to that point, a preliminary, *purposeful* step had to be undertaken: a forceful pruning exercise. The need to feed must have expressly and specifically been excised and bracketed. If this step is not taken, if the need for nutrition is embraced, then a quite different take on things ensues. Within this alternative strategy, the main trajectory is a shift from the centripetal to the centrifugal.

The stomach urges us outwards. It mandates that we move into our surroundings, engage with them, and revise and rework 'culture' – a term which now can be reconnected to its initial meaning of tilling the soil.

Overemphasis on mind can lead to detachment and a fascination with the realm of abstractions. The gastral, engaged in the various activities built around the root *cult*, tends towards the concrete. Those who *cult*ivate the soil and depend on its fruits for survival must, almost inevitably, be creatures of care. They find it hard to translate themselves into neutral, detached spectators. They seek out optimal ways of living, ways that manifest themselves in various *cult*ures. The surroundings in which they find themselves do not stand as mere neutral data. They are feature-laden, loci of signs, markers, possibilities and limitations. The sheer givenness of such conditions, when it gives rise to gratitude, can occasion yet another meaning of *cult*: reverence.

Hunger and the reflective practices required for appropriate feeding provide us with a fruitful context for reorienting our philosophies. Appetite re-emphasizes our continuity with the natural world. It makes us aware of our multiple connections and interdependencies: with the sun, soil, ants, bacteria, earthworms, plants as well as with other humans who grow, harvest, deliver and distribute foodstuffs. When a friend brings food to the house of someone who is ill, in mourning or otherwise in need, we would be inclined to say that this act was a 'thoughtful' one. Thoughtfulness is a term that fits neatly neither in the sequestered realm of pure rationality, nor in the arena of mere feeling. It is mixed and impure. As such, it better expresses the fully human activity at work in such acts of generosity. There is also thoughtfulness in answering the question 'how are we to eat?' We are reminded of the combinations emphasized in Chapter Two: nutrition, taste, ecological sustainability, economy and sociability must all be balanced against one another. The self-sufficient animal may be the 'rational' one, but the cooking animal, it turns out, is the thoughtful one.

Conclusion

Reconstructive Surgery

Mary Midgley once complained about 'moral surgeons' who cut out important parts of us.[1] In the West, the major amputation has excised the mind and elevated it to the status of 'philosophically relevant'. Much of philosophy in the West has taken for granted this post-surgical condition. A good life, on this scheme, is a maximally rational one. 'Rational', in turn, comes to be understood in opposition to what has been amputated: the affective, physiological, emotional and experiential sides of life. The task of this book has been to engage in reconstructive surgery. We have sought to bring back into philosophical significance just what is significant in ordinary life: that humans are integrated creatures whose emotional, affective, intelligent, social dimensions must somehow work together. The table has been our focus, and we have re-anointed humans as 'stomach-endowed', a naming that deliberately displaces the older focus on pure rationality. Reflecting on what it means to be stomach-endowed offers a new 'generative idea'; that is, a fruitful intellectual seed promising to germinate in ways quite different from that of a landscape seeded with the older focal idea of dualism.

The earlier guiding idea has had a good run. It has certainly been successful. Ordinary speech is replete with phrasings deriving from it: subjective versus objective, art versus craft, knowledge versus opinion, absolutism versus relativism, rational versus emotional, value versus fact, to identify the most prominent.

It has also helped create a landscape that in many ways is welcome and helpful. Humans are complicated. Thinking in terms of mind and body offers one way to get a handle on that complicatedness. Culturally, advances in science and technology along with the establishment of durable democratic republics have been among the most prominent flowerings associated with the epoch that opened with the Renaissance and received a major philosophical boost from Descartes.

At the same time, the motivating idea and its offspring contained limitations that began to emerge more fully as time progressed. Humans have always had a penchant for domination and control. And the world view that neatly sorted out things into matter on one hand and mind on the other provided a great foundation for domination and control. The natural world, including its animal denizens, now belonged to a category – matter – that was value-free. Meaning was to be found solely within mind. Whatever made up the rest of our surroundings could be transformed into 'stuff' to be shaped and manipulated for human use. Any lingering 'animistic' notions that would have granted some inherently worthwhile status to non-human entities began to fade away. 'Matter' itself lost its etymological associations with *mater*, mother, something deserving respect and gratitude. The '*moral* surgery' ended up being kind of *immoral*, making things easier for a human ethic of domination and control.

At the same time, another human temptation, that towards purity, came to be exacerbated. The great Enlightenment philosopher Immanuel Kant entitled his most famous work *Critique of Pure Reason*. If the stomach side of things was associated with hungers and the combinations of foods and recipes needed to satisfy those hungers, it necessarily represented mixture and combination. The mind, in its exalted state, could consider itself above all that. Combinations, amalgams and blends came automatically to have connotations of that which is lesser, that which is worse. Biologists may have identified the result of mixing and blending as 'heterosis', or hybrid vigour, a sign of health in animals.

Fans of purity, though, were quick to dismiss the 'mongrel' and 'miscegenation' in the human sphere. The temptation towards purity was nothing new. What emerged as new was the great impetus provided by the amputation of body from mind.

Another typical temptation is that of ducking out on responsibility and its accompaniment, anxiety. For a philosopher of the ancient world like Aristotle, human goodness was tied to 'practical wisdom' or 'prudential judgements', labels that in effect mean that in the end, some human element must be factored in to get things right. As long as the 'human element' and 'getting things right' are held together, anxiety is inescapable. It is neither possible to escape to a realm in which one just follows a formula or dictate (skipping the human element), nor to a realm in which all morality is subjective and in which you can just make up the rules as you go along (skipping the 'get it right' element).

As the twentieth century unfolded, the accumulated limitations of the older orientation manifested themselves in multiple and often disastrous ways, from racial extermination to ecological degradation, to radical oppositions between absolutists and relativists. At the midpoint in that century, the American philosopher Susanne Langer (1895–1985) summarized the situation this way: the 'springs of philosophic thought have run dry once more'. The guiding notions built around the axis of bifurcation 'have served their term'; 'the difficulties inherent in their constitutive concepts balk us now; their paradoxes clog our thinking. If we would have new knowledge, we must get us a whole world of new questions.'[2] Much twentieth-century philosophy was an effort to move towards new questions. Langer's own attempt took as its starting point the notion of symbolism. She saw this as a way of healing ruptures, as a way of bridging the gap between pure rationality, imagination and myth. From our perspective, such a move, helpful as it was, preserved the understanding of philosophy as fully and merely ensconced within mind and its activities. Arriving at a new set of formulations and questions – formulations and questions more consistent with the human condition – requires, as readers will by now realize, a more decisive step. The amputation that undergirded the preceding epoch has to be reversed. Such a reversal, we believe, can best be attained not by simply paying attention to the 'body' instead of to the 'mind'. Such a formulation itself continues to work within the bifurcated trajectory. Rather, a more promising approach would take the activities associated with the stomach as central, activities that are necessarily integrative, implicating as they do intelligence, memory, imagination and interaction with the biosphere.

This brief book sketches the results of that paradigm switch. It starts from a multi-dimensional question, 'how are we to eat?', and investigates the various ramifications of that question from the perspective of philosophy. The actual word 'philosophy' means 'love of wisdom'. Philosophy encompasses the human search for wisdom in its widest sense. That search is meaningless apart from the provision of some general cluster of questions whose treatment provides guidance in action. Those formulations provide some channels within which thinking can take place. As we have seen, the results of older philosophies become sedimented and taken for granted as the only ways to address a situation. Few people systematically examine the received formulations. Except philosophers, that is; that is their work. Their role is to suggest new motivating perspectives, new generative ideas. These in turn open up new channels for the search for wisdom.

Our new channel is symbolized by a specifically chosen representative figure. For us, the farmer replaces both the geometer and the spectator as the type most emblematic of the human condition. We know, we know: the very word 'farmer', given the inherited philosophical context, is, if not pejorative, then at least less than exalted. The word does not come with the halo of exaltation that accompanies, say, 'physicist', 'investment banker' or 'diplomat'. That, though, is precisely our point. Exaltation and dismissal do not just pop out of nowhere. It is time, we think, to refashion intellectual contours and allow farmers their due. For our purposes, this new representative figure offers important advantages.

The farmer, first of all, is an engaged participant, not a detached observer. Second, the farmer, in the traditional sense at least, oversees a setting marked by mixture – a jumble of animals, plants, soil conditions and the weather. Third, farmers cannot avoid the anxiety associated with prudential decisions. They pay heed to the counsel of experience, the latest scientific discoveries, weather reports, various techniques for pest control; but, in the end, there is a gap between all of this and the final decision they must make: to plant now, in this way, with or without these chemicals. Practical judgements are unavoidable, as is the risk of being wrong. It is quite appropriate to say 'it's up to the individual' to decide, but this does not mean 'it's up to the individual' whether that decision is the optimal one or not. The responsibility/ anxiety axis remains inescapable.

If at one end there is a direct line from the stomach to the farmer, at the other there is a line from the stomach to the table. The table is, most often, a shared place for sating the demands of the stomach. Among the issues layered into the question 'how are we to eat?' is that of who gets to share our table. Hospitality, in other words, gets revalorized. Within the older setting, the position that has been taken for granted is that hospitality is a matter of entertaining friends, or perhaps, in a business setting, a matter of the hospitality industry. We question that position. Hungry humans abound. Homes and houses have limited capacities. Ethics in such a setting takes on a concrete turn. How open will our houses be? How generous will we be in providing a place at table? In this way, philosophy joins economics and ecology, two fields whose names emerge from the Greek word for home or household (*oikos*). The central ethical question now becomes 'what kind of home are we making?'

The table is also a place for enjoyment, for creativity, for moments of ritual and celebration. Artistry, in such a context, takes on a different meaning from what it once had. The position taken for granted within the older scheme: 'art' is limited to what is produced for contemplation in a museum. But modes of approach circulating around the stomach can no longer privilege the purified, rarefied realm of the museum. Instead of emphasizing what is purely 'aesthetic', that category is now understood in terms of mixing, of combination. Fineness in artistry results when multiple dimensions can be combined in smooth and harmonious ways. The 'aesthetic', in addition, now comes to be associated with the entire situation, not with that of a single subject confronting an artwork in an artificial space. Does the situation, as its ingredients blend, mix and interact, occasion experience in which energies coalesce and come to some kind of harmonious culmination? To the degree that the answer is 'yes', the experience can be defined as aesthetic.

The possibilities of what can be brought to the table are vast. Not all are delectable. How do we know the difference? Traditional philosophy tells us that there is the realm of fact (is) and that of value (ought). A food can be described and, subsequently, someone can pronounce 'I like it' or 'I don't like it.' When we add stomach-centred questions beyond the delectable, questions such as whether something is digestible or poisonous, things get a bit more complicated – a complication that retroactively impacts even the case of delectability. We establish that foods are delectable, digestible or poisonous as the result of investigations that allow us to appreciate how the features of such foods react with our physiologies. Objectivity becomes responsibility, the concerted effort to arrive at justifiable beliefs. In some cases the emphasis will be more on the side of personal preference, in other cases it will be on the features of the possible foodstuffs. In general, though, it is the interaction, the combination of features and physiology, not the separation of fact from value that will be the rule. Speaking in ways that set up a clean contrast of knowledge (certain, objective) versus opinion (social construction, subjective) can no longer be accepted as the norm. Although within the older scheme of things it may seem counterintuitive, to describe knowing thus, in the everyday sense, it has much in common with tasting. Tasting is a kind of testing and as such offers a model for knowing.

The stomach, beneficiary of good recipes ingested, cannot be thought of as isolated, self-sufficient. It must be part of a context, of a setting in which possibilities of satiation are present. All formulations that begin with single, separate, auto-sufficient entities, formulations quite common in the standard philosophical context, are out of bounds for a perspective that takes the stomach seriously. 'With' is an ever-present preposition. In the older intellectual landscape, dependency and neediness are inevitably labelled deficiencies. The revised horizon revalorizes them. Overdependence and desperate neediness continue to be problematic, but simple dependence and neediness are descriptors of our condition, important descriptors that need to be taken into account, not simply dismissed. Seeking out the proper sorts of interdependencies, not seeking to avoid interdependency, now becomes a prime desideratum.

Philosophy has long prided itself in being the champion of rationality. But who, this book asks, made rationality king? It was the cluster of older, controlling ideas. When we take the stomach seriously, other terms can be rehabilitated. 'Rationality' remains fully situated within the context of 'moral surgery', which separates it from other dimensions of human life. Dethroning rationality does not mean a slide into irrationality. Such an either/or opposition works only within the earlier construal. The stomach, grounded as it is in everyday practices, needs *intelligence*, seeks *reasonableness*, does not disavow *thinking*. Indeed, when the stomach is grateful for the bounty that allows its satiation, its thanking is, as the writer Margaret Visser points out, an incipient form of thinking.[3] The thinking–thanking connection had earlier been identified by Heidegger. The words are related etymologically because both identify a human response to our circumstances. Thanking requires the acknowledgement of what is involved in a particular setting. 'Acknowledgement', as the word indicates, includes a particular kind of knowledge, an awareness that results from reflecting on the meaning of a scene. There is no thanking without thinking. Thinking, in turn, is one way in which humans give thanks, a mode of responding to our circumstances that recognizes the opportunities provided by them. The detached neutrality associated with rationality is recognized as an artificial, forced position. The acceptance of situatedness, including opportunities for reflection, roots the situation of thinking. There is no thinking without thanking. Philosophers, at least those at table, do not stand apart from the world and look out at it from an artificial perspective of enforced rationality. Instead, they are engaged participants whose interactions are naturally thankful and thoughtful.

References

Introduction

1   Liz Else, 'Mary, Mary, Quite Contrary', *New Scientist*, 2315
    (3 November 2001), www.newscientist.com.
2   Mary Midgley, *Utopias, Dolphins and Computers: Problems of
    Philosophical Plumbing* (London, 1996), p. 1.
3   Ibid.
4   Ibid., p. 2.
5   The American philosopher Charles Peirce called this the 'method of
    tenacity', and he had considerable admiration for it. He suggested
    that the capacity to put on blinders and refuse to acknowledge any
    alternative views was a method of establishing beliefs whose merits
    were inferior only to the scientific method. He wasn't kidding.
    Philosopher of science Paul Feyerabend suggested that ignoring
    – not refuting – alternative views is exactly what science does,
    science at its best. In a less polemical way, his fellow philosopher
    of science Thomas Kuhn suggested that science 'progresses' in
    a kind of galumphing alternation between 'normal science' – a
    period during which our most basic plumbing works are taken
    as given and correct, and in which repair projects are confined to
    installing new fixtures and repairing faucets – and 'revolutionary
    science', periods in which an irresolvable problem causes an entire
    system to be called into question. It is only during these periods
    of paradigm shift that the most elemental assumptions can be
    examined and disputed. Kuhn notes that normal scientists will
    hobble along for a very long time with a system that isn't answering
    some of their most pressing questions before they will resort to a

reconsideration of their most foundational beliefs. The more people invested in a system, the more likely it will be preserved despite the seriousness of its limitations. Note that there is nothing the least bit paradoxical about such an approach. On the contrary, the alternative is the paradoxical move.

6 Midgley, *Utopias*, p. 2.
7 Ibid., p. 11.
8 Ibid., p. 13.
9 Ibid., p. 3.
10 Ibid., p. 14.
11 Ibid.
12 Susanne Langer, *Philosophical Sketches* (New York, 1964), p. 13.
13 Susanne Langer, *Philosophy in a New Key* (Cambridge, MA, 1957), p. 293.
14 See John Dewey, *The Quest for Certainty*, in *The Later Works* (Carbondale, IL, 1929; 1984), vol. IV.
15 John Dewey, *Democracy and Education* (New York, 1922), pp. 335–6.
16 Sandor Katz, *The Art of Fermentation* (White River Junction, VT, 2012).
17 Ibid., p. xviii.
18 Ibid., pp. xviii–xix.

1 Hospitality is Ethics

1 Jessica Bruder, 'The Picky Eater who Came to Dinner', www.nytimes.com, 29 June 2012.
2 An actual headline: Jim Thornton, 'Is This the Most Dangerous Food for Men?', www.menshealth.com, 19 May 2009.
3 Michael Pollan, *The Omnivore's Dilemma: A Natural History of Four Meals* (New York, 2006), p. 314.
4 Jessica Bruder, 'Feeding Others' Food Issues', www.timesunion.com, 6 July 2012.
5 We have borrowed the notion of 'generative idea' from Susanne Langer, *Philosophy in a New Key* (Cambridge, MA, 1957).
6 Lisa Heldke, 'Foodmaking as a Thoughtful Practice', in *Cooking, Eating, Thinking: Transformative Philosophies of Food*, ed. Deane W. Curtin and Lisa Heldke (Indianapolis, IN, 1992), p. 203.

7   Here is a typical passage from Aristotle: 'By virtue I mean
    virtue of character; for this [pursues the mean because] it is
    concerned with feelings and actions, and these admit of excess,
    deficiency and an intermediate condition. We can be afraid,
    e.g., or be confident, or have appetites, or get angry, or feel pity,
    in general have pleasure or pain, both too much and too little,
    and in both ways not well; but [having these feelings] at the
    right times, about the right things, towards the right people,
    for the right end, and in the right way, is the intermediate and
    best condition, this is proper to virtue. Similarly, actions also
    admit of excess, deficiency and the intermediate condition.'
    See Aristotle, *Nicomachean Ethics*, trans. Terrence Irwin
    (Indianapolis, IN, 1985), 1106b: pp. 18–24.
8   Donna Gabaccia, *We Are What We Eat: Ethnic Food and the
    Making of Americans* (Cambridge, MA, 1998), p. 125.
9   Ibid., pp. 124, 123.
10 Ibid., p. 125.
11 Ibid., p. 126.
12 Ibid., p. 125.
13 Ibid., p. 127.
14 Emmanuel Levinas, *Totality and Infinity: An Essay on Exteriority*,
    trans. Alfonso Lingis (Pittsburgh, PA, 1961), is one of the most
    prominent.
15 See Henri Bergson, *The Two Sources of Morality and Religion*,
    trans. R. Ashley Audra and Cloudesley Brereton (Garden City,
    NJ, 1932; 1956).
16 Annia Ciezadlo, *Day of Honey: A Memoir of Food, Love, and War*
    (New York, 2011), p. 77.
17 William Bryant Logan, *Dirt: The Ecstatic Skin of the Earth*
    (New York, 1995), pp. 18–19.
18 Ibid., p. 19.
19 Of course, in offering the farmer as representative figure, we do
    not mean to suggest that all farmers are virtuous.
20 Some philosophers who challenged this ideal were Charles
    Sanders Peirce (1839–1914), Ludwig Wittgenstein (1889–1951)
    and William James (1842–1910).
21 Homer, *The Odyssey*, trans. Robert Fagles (New York, 1996),
    pp. 100–101.

22 Ibid., pp. 195–6.

23 Homer, *The Iliad*, trans. Richard Lattimore (Chicago, IL, 1961), pp. 119ff.

24 'In other words, there would be an antinomy, an insoluble antinomy, a non-dialectizable antinomy between, on the one hand, *The* law of unlimited hospitality (to give the new arrival all of one's home and oneself, to give him or her one's own, our own, without asking a name, or compensation, or the fulfilment of even the smallest condition), and on the other hand, the laws (in the plural), those rights and duties that are always conditioned and conditional, as they are defined by the Greco-Roman tradition and even the Judeo-Christian one, by all of law and all philosophy of law up to Kant and Hegel in particular, across the family, civil society, and the state . . . The tragedy, for it is a tragedy of destiny, is that the two antagonistic terms of this antinomy are not symmetrical. There is a strange hierarchy in this. *The* law is above the laws . . . But even while keeping itself above the laws of hospitality, *the* unconditional law of hospitality needs the laws, it *requires* them. The demand is constitutive. It wouldn't be effectively unconditional, the law, if it didn't *have to become* effective, concrete, determined, if that were not its being as having-to-be. It would risk being abstract, utopian, illusory, and so turning over into its opposite. In order to be what it is, *the* law thus needs the laws, which, however, deny it, or at any rate threaten it, sometimes corrupt or pervert it. And must always be able to do this.' See Anne Dufourmantelle and Jacques Derrida, *Of Hospitality*, trans. Rachel Bowlby (Stanford, CA, 2000), pp. 77, 79.

25 'Hierocles, a Stoic of the first–second centuries AD (using an older metaphor found also in Cicero's *De Officiis*), argued that we should regard ourselves not as devoid of local affiliations, but as surrounded by a series of concentric circles. The first one is drawn around the self; the next takes in one's immediate family; then follows the extended family; then, in order, one's neighbours or local group, one's fellow city-dwellers, one's fellow countrymen. Outside all these circles is the largest one, that of humanity as a whole. Our task as citizens of the world will be to "draw the circles somehow toward the centre," making all

human beings more like our fellow city dwellers, and so forth.'
See Martha Nussbaum, 'Kant and Stoic Cosmopolitanism',
The Journal of Political Philosophy, v/1 (1997), p. 9.

26 Lincoln Steffens, quoted in Henry Steele Commager,
Introduction to Jane Addams, *Twenty Years at Hull House*
(New York, 1910), p. x.

27 Addams, *Twenty Years at Hull House*, pp. 98 (solidarity), 55
(justice), 76 (reciprocity).

28 Ibid., p. 59.

29 Ibid., p. xviii.

30 Ibid.

31 Ibid., p. 169. The word 'better' here rings harshly on the
contemporary ear; Addams does indeed mean Americans
of a more privileged class.

32 Ibid., p. 96.

33 Ibid., p. 67.

II Food as/and Art

1 Adam Gopnik, 'Sweet Revolution', www.newyorker.com,
3 January 2011.

2 'Freestyle Cooking', www.cellercanroca.com, accessed
24 January 2014.

3 Alice Waters, 'A Delicious Revolution', www.ecoliteracy.org,
accessed 15 January 2014.

4 Wendell Berry, 'The Pleasures of Eating', www.ecoliteracy.org,
accessed 15 January 2014.

5 Hervé This, *Building a Meal: From Molecular Gastronomy to
Culinary Constructivism*, trans. M. B. DeBevoise (New York,
2009), p. 99.

6 Laura Marks, 'Thinking Multisensory Culture', *Paragraph*,
xxxi/2 (2008), p. 124.

7 G.W.F. Hegel, *Aesthetics: Lectures on Fine Art*, trans. T. M. Knox
(Oxford, 1998), vol. 1, p. 36.

8 Annie Churdar, 'Unbelievable Sushi Art by Takayo Kiyota',
www.lostateminor.com, 23 September 2013.

9 What is interesting for Kant, and a good object lesson in
how terms gather significance in terms of their philosophical

setting, is how he fastens on the word 'taste' but in a way that has nothing to do with tasting at table. '*Taste* is the faculty for judging an object or a kind of representation through a satisfaction or dissatisfaction *without any interest*. The object of such a satisfaction is called *beautiful*.' (Immanuel Kant, *Critique of the Power of Judgement*, trans. Paul Guyer and Eric Matthews (Cambridge, 2000), p. 96, emphases in original). The first paragraphs of the first section, called 'Critique of Aesthetic Judgement', stress disinterest and universality while dismissing the aesthetic relevance of food and drink, as well as of ethical judgements. Food falls within the category of the 'agreeable', which is always combined with interest, the kiss of death for Kantian aesthetics. When Kant writes of 'a dish that stimulates the taste through spices and other flavourings, one may say without hesitation that it is agreeable' (p. 93), he is closing the door on the possibility of food entering the realm of real beauty and thus the aesthetic.

10 Kandinsky, for instance, believed that colour had the capacity to directly touch the soul itself – in the presence of what is truly 'artistic', 'the spectator finds a sympathetic vibration within his own soul.' See Wassily Kandinsky, *Concerning the Spiritual in Art* [1912], in *Kandinsky: Complete Writings on Art*, ed. Kenneth C. Lindsay and Peter Vergo (New York, 1994), p. 129.

11 For another philosophical take on the aesthetics of food, among other topics, see Elizabeth Telfer, *Food for Thought* (London and New York, 2002).

12 Carolyn Korsmeyer, *Making Sense of Taste: Food and Philosophy* (Ithaca, NY, 1999), p. 136.

13 Ibid., p. 144.

14 Ibid., p. 143.

15 Ibid., p. 144.

16 Ibid.

17 See, for instance, John Dewey, *Art as Experience* (New York, 1958).

18 There are of course 'difficult aesthetic pleasures', such as disgust. Korsmeyer has also written about these. See Carolyn Korsmeyer, *Savoring Disgust: The Foul and the Fair in Aesthetics* (Oxford and New York, 2011).

19 Jean Anthelme Brillat-Savarin, *The Physiology of Taste*, www.gutenberg.org.
20 'Viviane Le Courtois: Edible? Twenty-two years of Working with Food', Boulder Museum of Contemporary Art, www.bmoca.org, accessed 15 January 2014.
21 William Deresiewicz, 'A Matter of Taste', www.nytimes.com, 26 October 2012.
22 Aaron Meskin, 'The Art of Food', *The Philosophers' Magazine* (July 2013), pp. 81–6.
23 Quoted in Warren Belasco, *Food: The Key Concepts* (London, 2008), p. 47.
24 William Deresiewicz, 'Soul Food: Why Cooking isn't Art', www.theamericanscholar.org, accessed 16 January 2014.

III Tasting, Testing, Knowing

1 See Mary Midgley, *Beast and Man: The Roots of Human Nature* (Ithaca, NY, 1978), p. 14.
2 The second *sapiens* in the name *Homo sapiens sapiens* indicates that (at least according to some archaeologists) we modern humans are a subspecies of the species *Homo sapiens*. According to these specialists, there are other (archaic, extinct) subspecies of our species, including *Homo sapiens idaltu* and *Homo sapiens neanderthalensis*. On other schools of thought, these archaic beings were in fact different species, not different subspecies, and we modern humans are the only members of the species, making us just plain *Homo sapiens*, not *Homo sapiens sapiens*. No matter; we're still the tasting species.
3 Adam Drewnowski, professor of epidemiology at the University of Washington, is the researcher cited in Michael Moss, *Salt, Sugar, Fat: How the Food Giants Hooked Us* (New York, 2013), p. 156.
4 Asking about the apportionment of blame, subsequent to gathering all empirical evidence, Hume has this to say: 'The approbation or blame which then ensues, cannot be the work of the judgment, but of the heart; and is not a speculative proposition or affirmation, but an active feeling or sentiment.' See David Hume, *An Inquiry into the Principles of Morals* (Lasalle, 1777), Appendix 1, p. 131.

5   There exists a whole category of aesthetic experiences that are
    rooted in risk and danger. Some years ago, the fugu (pufferfish)
    craze swept the media, if not the dining tables of most of it.
    Fugu must be cleaned and prepared in a very precise way, or the
    toxins located in one of its bodily organs are released and it will
    kill the eater. For a certain class of thrill-seeker, this additional
    danger contributes to the pleasure in the dining experience.

6   To the extent that we can accept the distinction as legitimate,
    we'd say instead that it's more about whether we understand
    there to be a separation between the thing and the sensation it
    causes. Consider: in the case of fresh, hot bread, it makes sense
    to us to say that the bread *is* that thing to which we point. We
    would not similarly say the fresh bread *is* its smell. To what
    extent is this simply a matter of ostention, of pointing? You
    can't point to anything except images. Are there other similar
    bodily gestures associated with all the senses? How do you
    help someone tease out the specific taste you are tasting? How
    is it like or unlike having someone figure out what bird you're
    pointing to on which branch? You can be 'sure(ish)' with the
    bird. How can you be sure with a taste or smell?

7   See Thomas Nagel, *The View from Nowhere* (New York, 1989).

8   M.F.K. Fisher describes an astonishing lunch she had one day
    in a small restaurant in a tiny French town. One of the courses
    of this miraculous meal included trout, which were prepared
    tableside. She seems rather delighted – in a horrified sense – by
    their death agony. Her server, who is the ostensible subject of
    this essay, 'I was Really Very Hungry', says of the trout: 'Any
    trout is glad, truly glad to be prepared by Monsieur Paul. His
    little gills are pinched, with one flash of the knife he is empty,
    and then he curls in agony in the bouillon and it is over.'
    Fisher's description of the trout's choices makes it sound almost
    like one of those late-night college conversations in which you
    contemplate whether you would rather die in a car accident or of
    a slow but not too painful cancer; it almost seems as if the trout
    has been consulted, and found to prefer a quick, albeit hideously
    painful death to a long, slow suffocation in a polluted trout
    stream. See M.F.K. Fisher, *The Gastronomical Me* (New York,
    1943; 1989), pp. 144–5.

9   In his encyclopaedic work on fermentation, *The Art of Fermentation*, Sandor Katz devotes considerable attention to describing the range of ways that a particular fermented food might present to our noses, tongues and eyes, both because many of these foods are unfamiliar to us, and because we are particularly skittish about foods that are fermented, a category many contemporary Americans tend to conflate with 'rotten'. 'Is it really supposed to smell like that?' is a pretty important question to ask, especially if the 'it' in question is the thigh of a deer you have cured. Such foods are not without their dangers. See Sandor Katz, *Wild Fermentation: The Flavor, Nutrition, and Craft of Live-culture Foods* (White River Junction, VT, 2003).

10 This discussion assumes vision. For philosophically rich discussions of the ways in which the role of, and relationships among, the senses are organized for a visually impaired person, see 'The Blind Cook', www.theblindcook.com, accessed 21 January 2014.

11 David Sutton, in Carolyn Korsmeyer and David Sutton, 'The Sensory Experience of Food', *Food, Culture and Society*, xiv/4 (December 2011), p. 469.

12 Ibid., pp. 468, 470.

13 A passage in Alexander McCall Smith's book invites reflection on the role that memory and emotion can or could play. Cyril the dog is taken by his owner on a trip to Italy. In a chapter entitled 'The Impact of Italy', McCall Smith invites readers to experience Italy from a 'dog's nose' perspective:

> The smells, of course, were quite different from those attendant on a comparable Scottish journey, and none of the human passengers had even the faintest inkling of how exciting was the olfactory tapestry that Cyril now enjoyed. The world as it reveals itself to the canine nose is far richer than we can possibly imagine, and includes not only that which is there – which is interesting enough – but also that which was there before; so, while the human eye may see signs of the impact of man – farm walls, grain towers, well-worked farms – the dog picks up so much more: historic scents that have been layered upon the landscape and have not gone away. We, then, may

look at a Tuscan field and see furrows, stones, dry white earth; this would be thin fare for the dog, who will know that those furrows were ploughed by oxen, that birds had pecked at the seed sown by the farmer whose boots in turn left behind them a story quite of their own, of tramping upon a cellar floor, of walking amongst olive trees, and of so much else. All this Cyril now picked up and relished, quivering with excitement at the intellectual challenge of interpreting and classifying this bewildering array of scents.

Cyril's experience of smells is more than an acknowledgement of what's there at the moment; smell for him stretches into the past, encompassing what used to be there as well. Smelling becomes deeply relational and, as a result, less about the 'proximate' versus the 'distal' (smelling seems to split the difference here). Granting the passage's fancifulness, it nevertheless leads us to ask how our different senses manifest, or involve us in, relationality differently from each other. See Alexander McCall Smith, *The Importance of Being Seven* (New York, 2012), p. 235.

14 Lisa Heldke and Stephen Kellert, 'Objectivity as Responsibility', *Metaphilosophy*, XXVI/4 (1995), pp. 360–78.

15 John Dewey, 'Logic: The Theory of Inquiry', in *The Later Works* (Carbondale, IL, 1938; 1991), vol. XII, p. 108.

16 Of course not all humans chew and swallow food. Many human beings take their nutrients in other ways, because they have been disabled from eating. The film critic Roger Ebert wrote a powerful essay entitled 'Nil By Mouth', which chronicles his life as a person who takes his nutriment in another way. See Roger Ebert, 'Nil by Mouth', www.rogerebert.com, 6 January 2010.

17 Heidegger explores this question in his essay 'The Question Concerning Technology'. See Martin Heidegger, 'The Question Concerning Technology', in *The Question Concerning Technology and Other Essays*, trans. William Lovitt (New York, 1977).

18 Plato, *The Timaeus*, trans. Benjamin Jowett, http://classics.mit.edu/Plato/timaeus.html, 72e–73a, accessed 21 January 2014.

19 John Dewey, *The Later Works, 1925–1953*, vol. I: *1925, Experience and Nature* (*Colleted Works of John Dewey*), electronic edition, p. 212.

20 John Dewey, *The Quest for Certainty*, in *The Later Works*, vol. IV,
    p. 4.
21 Ibid., p. 5.

IV Being Hungry, Hungry Being

1   Jessica Jacobs, 'The Evo Diet', www.livestrong.com, accessed
    3 December 2013.
2   Sheryl Walters, 'Eat Like the Apes for Optimum Health',
    www.naturalnews.com, 29 November 2008.
3   Jacobs, 'The Evo Diet'.
4   See Barfworld, www.barfworld.com.
5   Richard Wrangham, *Catching Fire: How Cooking Made Us
    Human* (New York, 2010), p. 25.
6   Aristotle, *De Anima*, trans. J. A. Smith, http://classics.mit.edu/
    Aristotle/soul.html, 413 1, 1–4.
7   The *Oxford English Dictionary* entry on 'self' indicates the word's
    history as that of a pronoun, an adjective and then a noun. The
    seventeenth-century usage, illustrated by a passage from Locke,
    is introduced this way: 'Chiefly *Philos.* That which in a person
    is really and intrinsically *he* (in contradistinction to what is
    adventitious); the ego (often identified with the soul or mind
    as opposed to the body); a permanent subject of successive and
    varying states of consciousness.'
8   See W. H. Auden, 'Tonight at Seven-thirty (For M.F.K. Fisher)'
    (1963). Available online at http://gastrocentric.blogspot.co.uk,
    accessed 30 September 2015.
9   Jean-Marie Pelt, *La Raison du plus faible* (Paris, 2009),
    p. 59.
10 For a fascinating description, see 'Tom Volk's Fungus of the
    Month for October 2002', http://botit.botany.wisc.edu, accessed
    22 January 2014.
11 See the BBC programme 'Frontiers: Human Microbes',
    www.bbc.co.uk, 1 June 2011.
12 For Diogenes the Sinope, see Diogenes Laertius, *Lives of the
    Philosophers,* ed. R. D. Hicks, vol. VI, www.perseus.tufts.edu/
    hopper. For Crates and Hipparchia see 'Hipparchia',
    www.iep.utm.edu, accessed 22 January 2014.

13 Henry Fielding, *The History of Tom Jones* (New York, 1749; 1950), p. 11.

14 Jean-Jacques Rousseau, *On the Social Contract*, trans. Donald A. Cress (Indianapolis, IN, 1762), p. 17.

15 Jean-Jacques Rousseau, *Émile; or, On Education*, trans. Allan Bloom (New York, 1762b), p. 37.

16 Ibid., p. 63.

17 Ibid.

18 Ibid., p. 151.

19 See 'Am I Hungry? is the END of Yo-yo Dieting', www.amihungry.com, accessed 22 January 2014.

20 Rousseau, *Émile*, pp. 151–2.

21 Ibid., p. 156.

22 Jean-Jacques Rousseau, *Discourse on the Origin of Inequality*, trans. Donald A. Cress (Indianapolis, IN, 1755), pp. 19–20.

23 Ibid., p. 19.

24 Ibid.

25 Ibid., p. 23.

26 Ibid., p. 25.

27 Ibid., pp. 25–6.

28 The nineteenth-century painter Paul Gauguin revealed the limits of Rousseau's nature/culture divide, however, when he described his experience of coming to Tahiti. Gauguin realized that food surrounded him, in abundance, but he had none of the (technological) capabilities needed to procure it for himself. Were he not possessed of a wallet, and were he not surrounded by knowledgeable native people, he would have been in a bind. Rousseau's belief that one can satisfy one's hungers 'naturally', without the aid of any (culturally created) technologies, strikes one as awfully naive when one gives it the least consideration.

29 Rousseau, *Discourse*, p. 26.

30 Ibid., p. 29.

31 One not surprising corollary: the agriculture/culture amalgamation, not the nature/culture opposition, was taken for granted.

32 Rousseau, *Discourse,* p. 34.

33 Ibid., p. 36.

34 Ibid., p. 39.

35 Ibid., p. 57.
36 Charles Guignon, *On Being Authentic* (New York, 2004), p. 55.
37 Ibid., pp. 59, 67.
38 Ibid., p. 60.
39 Michael Tsarion, 'Authentic Lives', www.youtube.com, uploaded 19 August 2009, accessed 21 July 2015.
40 Clifford Geertz, 'The Impact of the Concept of Culture on the Concept of Man', in *New Views of the Nature of Man*, ed. John R. Platt (Chicago, IL, 1965), p. 27.
41 George Santayana, 'Introduction' to *The Life of Reason*, in *The Essential Santayana*, comp. with an introduction by Martin A. Coleman (Bloomington, IN, 2009), p. 291.
42 The point brings to mind Aristotle's discussion of matter and form. See, for instance, his *Metaphysics*, Book VII.
43 Guignon, *On Being Authentic*, p. 105.
44 They do not do so necessarily; there is no guarantee that the back and forth will always bring a superior result. But generally, the results of this interaction will be superior to those produced in isolation.
45 For a brief and clear explanation of this, see Michael Pollan, *Cooked: A Natural History of Transformation* (New York, 2013), where he explains the thesis defended by Richard Wrangham in *Catching Fire: How Cooking Made Us Human* (New York, 2010).
46 Wrangham, *Catching Fire*, p. 182. Perhaps no animals cook, but many animals do exhibit preferences for some foods over others, and those preferences could be understood to amount to something like 'food preparation', even if they don't rise to the level of sophistication we would call 'cooking'. Animals, too, are by nature cultural.
47 This is not to say that there might not *be* particular cooking – or growing – practices that we term 'artificial', where that term is understood not in some absolute sense, but rather as a comparative. Twinkies and Skittles are – in some meaningful sense of the term – artificial.

Conclusion: Reconstructive Surgery

1   Mary Midgley, *Beast And Man: The Roots of Human Nature* (London, 1978), p. 166.
2   Susanne Langer, *Philosophy in a New Key* (Cambridge, MA, 1957), p. 13.
3   See Margaret Visser, *The Gift of Thanks: The Roots and Rituals of Gratitude* (Boston, MA, 2009), pp. 173, 235, 287–9.

Bibliography

Addams, Jane, *Twenty Years at Hull-House* [1910] (New York, 1981)

Alexanyan, S. M., and V. I. Krivchenko, 'Vavilov Institute Scientists
Heroically Preserve World Plant Genetic Resources Collections
During World War II Siege of Leningrad', *Diversity*, VII (1991),
pp. 10–13

Aristotle, *The Complete Works of Aristotle*, 2 vols, ed. Jonathan Barnes
(Princeton, NJ, 1984)

—, *Nicomachean Ethics*, trans. Terry Irwin (Indianapolis, IN, 1999)

Auden, W. H. 'Tonight at Seven-thirty (For M.F.K. Fisher)' [1936],
available at http://gastrocentric.blogspot.com, accessed 30
September 2015

Aurelius, Marcus, *The Meditations*, trans. G.M.A. Grube (Indianapolis,
IN, 1963)

Belasco, Warren, *Food: The Key Concepts* (London, 2008)

Bergson, Henri, *The Two Sources of Morality and Religion*, trans.
R. Ashley Audra and Cloudesley Brereton (Garden City, NJ, 1935)

Berry, Wendell, 'The Pleasures of Eating' [1989], available at www.
ecoliteracy.org, accessed 30 September 2015

Boisvert, Raymond, 'Cooking Up a New Philosophy', *The Philosophers'
Magazine*, LXI (2nd Quarter 2013), pp. 69–74

—, 'Food Transforms Philosophy', *The Maine Scholar*, XIV (2001),
pp. 1–14

—, 'Philosophy Regains its Senses', *Philosophy Now*, XXXI (2000),
pp. 9–11

Bordo, Susan, *Unbearable Weight: Feminism, Western Culture, and the
Body* (Berkeley, CA, 1993)

Brillat-Savarin, Jean Anthelme, *The Physiology of Taste; or, Transcendental Gastronomy* [1825], trans. Fayette Robinson, available at www.gutenberg.org, accessed 30 September 2015

Bruder, Jessica, 'Feeding Others' Food Issues', www.timesunion.com, 6 July 2012

Camus, Albert, *The Myth of Sisyphus*, trans. Justin O'Brien (New York, 1955)

Cicero, *Tusculan Disputations*, trans. J. E. King (Cambridge, MA, 1945)

Ciezadlo, Annia, *Day of Honey: A Memoir of Food, Love, and War* (New York, 2011)

Churdar, Annie, 'Unbelievable Sushi Art by Takayo Kiyota', www.lostateminor.com, 23 September 2013

Cox, Harvey, *On Not Leaving It to the Snake* (New York, 1967)

Deleuze, Gilles, and Félix Guattari, *What is Philosophy?*, trans. Hugh Tomlinson and Graham Burchell (New York, 1996)

Deresiewicz, William, 'Soul Food: Why Cooking Isn't Art', www.theamericanscholar.org, 25 November 2012

Derrida, Jacques, *Adieu to Emmanuel Levinas*, trans. Pascale-Anne Brault and Michael Naas (Stanford, CA, 1999)

—, *On Cosmopolitanism and Forgiveness*, trans. Mark Dooley and Michael Hughes (London, 2001)

—, and Anne Dufourmantelle, *Of Hospitality: Anne Dufourmantelle invites Jacques Derrida to Respond*, trans. Rachel Bowlby (Stanford, CA, 2000)

Dewey, John, *Art as Experience* [1934] (New York, 1958)

—, *The Later Works of John Dewey, 1925–1953*, vol. IV: *1929, The Quest for Certainty* (Carbondale, IL, 1984)

—, *The Later Works of John Dewey, 1925–1953*, vol. XII: *1938, Logic: The Theory of Inquiry* (Carbondale, IL, 1991)

Diogenes Laertius, *Lives of Eminent Philosophers*, vol. II, trans. R. D. Hicks (Cambridge MA, 1950)

Ebert, Roger, 'Nil by Mouth', www.rogerebert.com, 6 January 2010

El Celler de Can Roca, 'Freestyle Cooking', www.cellercanroca.com, accessed 24 January 2014

Fielding, Henry, *The History of Tom Jones* [1749] (New York, 1950)

Fields, Helen, 'How the Tree Frog has Redefined Our View of Biology', www.smithsonianmag.com, January 2013

Fisher, M.F.K., *The Gastronomical Me* [1943] (New York, 1989)

Frontiers, 'Human Microbes', BBC Radio 4, 1 June 2011, www.bbc.co.uk

Gabaccia, Donna, *We Are What We Eat: Ethnic Foods and the Making of Americans* (Cambridge, MA, 1998)

Geertz, Clifford, 'The Impact of the Concept of Culture on the Concept of Man', in *New Views of the Nature of Man*, ed. John R. Platt (Chicago, IL, 1965)

Gilbert, Elizabeth, *Eat, Pray, Love: One Woman's Search for Everything Across Italy, India and Indonesia* (New York, 2006)

Goldstein, Rebecca, *The Mind-Body Problem* (New York, 1993)

Gopnik, Adam, 'Sweet Revolution: The Power of the Pastry Chef', *The New Yorker* (3 January 2011), www.newyorker.com

Guignon, Charles, *On Being Authentic* (New York, 2004)

Hegel, G.W.F., *Aesthetics: Lectures on Fine Art*, trans. T. M. Knox (Oxford, 1975)

Heidegger, Martin, *The Question Concerning Technology and Other Essays*, trans. William Lovitt (New York, 1977)

Heldke, Lisa, *Exotic Appetites: Ruminations of a Food Adventurer* (New York, 2004)

—, 'Foodmaking as a Thoughtful Practice', in *Cooking, Eating, Thinking: Transformative Philosophies of Food*, ed. Deane W. Curtin and Lisa Heldke (Indianapolis, IN, 1992)

—, and Stephen Kellert, 'Objectivity as Responsibility', *Metaphilosophy*, XXVI (1995), pp. 360–78

Holmes, Seth, *Fresh Fruit, Broken Bodies: Migrant Farmworkers in the United States* (Berkeley, CA, 2013)

Homer, *The Iliad*, trans. Richmond Lattimore (Chicago, IL, 1961)

—, *The Odyssey*, trans. Robert Fagles (New York, 1996)

—, *The Odyssey*, trans. Stanley Lombardo (Indianapolis, IN, 2000)

Hume, David, *An Inquiry into the Principles of Morals* (LaSalle, IL, 1966)

Jablonka, Eva, and Marion Lamb, *Evolution in Four Dimensions: Genetic, Epigenetic, Behavioral, and Symbolic Variation in the History of Life* (Cambridge, MA, 2005)

James, William, *Pragmatism* (Indianapolis, IN, 1981)

Jones, Judith, *The Tenth Muse: My Life in Food* (New York, 2007)

Kandinsky, Wassily, 'Concerning the Spiritual in Art', in *Kandinsky: Complete Writings on Art*, ed. Kenneth C. Lindsay and Peter Vergo (New York, 1994)

Kant, Immanuel, *Critique of the Power of Judgment*, trans. Paul Guyer
and Eric Matthews (Cambridge, 2000)

Katz, Sandor, *Wild Fermentation: The Flavor, Nutrition, and Craft of
Live-culture Foods* (White River Junction, VT, 2003)

Koebler, Jason, 'Bacon Craze Hits Burger King Sundae',
www.usnews.com, 13 June 2012

Korsmeyer, Carolyn, *Making Sense of Taste: Food and Philosophy*
(Ithaca, NY, 1999)

—, *Savoring Disgust: The Foul and the Fair in Aesthetics* (Oxford and
New York, 2011)

Langer, Susanne, *Philosophy in a New Key*, 3rd edn (Cambridge,
MA, 1996)

Le Courtois, Viviane, 'Edible? Twenty-two years of Working With
Food', www.bmoca.org, accessed 15 January 2014

Levinas, Emmanuel, 'Ethics as First Philosophy', in *The Levinas Reader*,
ed. Seán Hand (London, 1989)

—, *Totality and Infinity: An Essay on Exteriority*, trans. Alfonso Lingis
(Pittsburgh, PA, 1961)

Lipkowitz, Ina, *Words to Eat By: Five Foods and the Culinary History
of the English Language* (New York, 2011)

Locke, John, *An Essay Concerning Human Understanding* [1689],
vol. I (New York, 1971)

Logan, William Bryant, *Dirt: The Ecstatic Skin of the Earth*
(New York, 1995)

McCall Smith, Alexander, *The Importance of Being Seven: The New 44
Scotland Street Novel* (New York, 2012)

Marks, Laura, 'Thinking Multisensory Culture', *Paragraph*, XXXI (2008),
pp. 123–37

Midgley, Mary, *Beast and Man* (Ithaca, NY, 1978)

—, *Utopias, Dolphins and Computers: Problems of Philosophical
Plumbing* (London, 1996)

Molière, *Amphitryon*, trans. Richard Wilbur (New York, 1995)

Moss, Michael, *Salt, Sugar, Fat: How the Food Giants Hooked Us*
(New York, 2013)

Nagel, Thomas, *The View from Nowhere* (New York, 1989)

Norman, Andy, 'The Machinery of Moral Progress: An Interview
with Rebecca Newberger Goldstein', www.thehumanist.com,
27 August 2014

Nussbaum, Martha, 'Kant and Stoic Cosmopolitanism', *The Journal of Political Philosophy*, V (1997), pp. 1–25

Ortega y Gasset, José, *What is Philosophy?*, trans. Mildred Adams (New York, 1960)

Partridge, Eric, *Origins: A Short Etymological Dictionary of Modern English* (New York, 1958)

Pasternak, Charles, *What Makes Us Human* (Oxford, 2007)

Pelt, Jean-Marie, *La Raison du plus faible* (Paris, 2009)

Plato, *Complete Works*, ed. John M. Cooper (Indianapolis, IN, 1997)

Pollan, Michael, *Cooked: A Natural History of Transformation* (New York, 2013)

—, *The Omnivore's Dilemma: A Natural History of Four Meals* (New York, 2006)

Poole, Steven, *You Aren't What You Eat* (London, 2013)

Popper, Karl, *Objective Knowledge* (Oxford, 1972)

Plato, *The Republic*, trans. G.M.A. Grube and C.D.C. Reeve (Indianapolis, IN, 1992)

Plutarch, 'On Exile', in *Plutarch's Moralia*, vol. VII, trans. Phillip H. De Lacy and Benedict Einarson (Cambridge, MA, 1959)

Roach, John, 'Bee Decline May Spell End for Some Fruits, Vegetables', www.nationalgeographic.com, 5 October 2004

Rorty, Richard, *Consequences of Pragmatism* (Minneapolis, MN, 1982)

Rossi, Paolo, *Manger: besoin, désir, obsession*, trans. Patrick Vighetti (Paris, 2012)

Rousseau, Jean-Jacques, *Émile; or, On Education*, trans. Allan Bloom (New York, 1979)

—, *Discourse on the Origin of Inequality*, trans. Donald A. Cress (Indianapolis, IN, 1992)

—, *On the Social Contract*, trans. Donald A. Cress (Indianapolis, IN, 1987)

Sartre, Jean-Paul, *Existentialism is a Humanism* [1946], trans. Carol Macomber (New Haven, CT, 2007)

Sellars, Wilfrid, 'Philosophy and the Scientific Image of Man', in *Frontiers of Science and Philosophy*, ed. Robert Colodny (Pittsburgh, PA, 1962)

Simmel, Georg, *The Sociology of Georg Simmel* (New York, 1950)

Telfer, Elizabeth, *Food for Thought: Philosophy and Food* (London, 1996)

This, Hervé, *Building a Meal: From Molecular Gastronomy to Culinary Constructivism*, trans. M. B. DeBevoise (New York, 2009)

Visser, Margaret, *The Gift of Thanks: The Roots and Rituals of Gratitude* (Boston, MA, 2009)

Volk, Thomas, 'Thomas Volk's Fungus of the Month: Oct. 2002', http://botit.botany.wisc.edu/toms_fungi, accessed 30 September 2015

Waters, Alice, 'Alice Waters Applies a "Delicious Revolution" to School Food', www.ecoliteracy.org, 29 June 2009

Woodbridge, Frederick J. E., *Nature and Mind: Selected Essays* [1937] (New York, 1965)

Wrangham, Richard, *Catching Fire: How Cooking Makes us Human.* (New York, 2010)

—, 'The Cooking Enigma', in *What Makes Us Human?*, ed. Charles Pasternak (Oxford, 2007)

Acknowledgements

Thank you to Andrew Smith, who generously made the initial connection between Reaktion Books and Lisa. Thanks to Michael Leaman at Reaktion for his editorial guidance with this project. Thank you also to the production staff at Reaktion for their meticulous attention to detail.

Portions of this work have been presented by one or both of us at the joint meetings of the Association for the Study of Food and Society, the Agriculture, Food and Human Values Society and at Occidental College. The authors are grateful for the feedback they received from audiences in both these venues.

Barbara Heldke read and commented on a draft of the entire manuscript, making many helpful suggestions for rendering it clearer and more coherent. We appreciate her time a great deal – and also her enthusiasm for the project. Krystal Bundy read and made extensive comments on an early draft of the Introduction. Ashley Steinberg put the references into proper format, a job that required careful attention to detail. Samantha Manick created the book's index, using her philosopher's eye and her baker's attention to detail.

Ray's writing was supported by a sabbatical from Siena College, by the college's reassigned time programme, and by the generous assignment of a library carrel. His wife, Jayne, besides being a constant source of food ideas, suggested spending the sabbatical in Paris, as good a place as any to write about food and philosophy.

Lisa's work on the book was aided considerably by the writing workshops that are held monthly at Gustavus Adolphus College, and are sponsored there by the John S. Kendall Center for Engaged Learning. These days of uninterrupted writing, carried out in the presence of colleagues doing the same thing, were absolutely essential to this work. Thanks to Alisa Rosenthal and Cathy Blaukat of the Kendall Center for coordinating them, and to the colleagues who shared those days with Lisa. She is also grateful to Béla Fleck and the Flecktones, whose music provided the soundtrack for her revisions. She thanks Peg O'Connor, who continues to influence her philosophy.

Index